Contents

Introduction

● Since time immemorial the Alessi family has been firmly established on Lake Orta. We originally come from Luzzogno, the oldest village in the Strona valley. The first Alessi I've traced was called Giovanni; in 1633 he married a certain Caterina Gozano in Luzzogno. That's all I know about him, and I don't know a great deal more about the eight generations separating him from me. I nonetheless have no doubt that my forebears were among the many men from the Strona valley who, in the seventeen hundreds, went as far as Germany to learn the trade of pewter-maker. Some of their number stayed on to make their fortune; others returned home and opened the first craft workshops. Such were the beginnings of the Omegna (and its suburb Crusinallo) makers of metal household objects, today one of the most dynamic centres in Europe for the production of such items.

▲ Six members of the Alessi family, each with one of our most famous "mystery objects", Philippe Starck's *Juicy Salif* lemon squeezer. Sitting in the centre is Carlo; behind him, his brother Ettore, son Michele and nephew Stefano; sitting to his left is his son Alessio. I'm the one in the foreground.

ALESSI

▲ The blue expanse of Lake Orta from above. Right, the outline of *Anna G.*, the character created by Alessandro Mendini as a corkscrew, watching over the Crusinallo plant.

▲ In the Strona valley, between the slopes of Monte Rosa and the lake, traditions retain a tenacious grip; a new museum, the Omegna Forum, gathers together the moving testimonies of centuries of toil and poetry.

The first metal household article manufacturer in the Cusio area was a man called Baldassare Cane, who towards the mid-eighteen hundreds had the courage to leave Chesio (another small village in the Strona valley) for the lakeside and found the first true workshop. Although the company no longer exists, by around 1900 it was a large employer. In the following years his example was followed by many dozens of craftsmen/small businessmen, who often learned their trade as workmen at Cane's factory. Over the course of one and a half centuries, pewter has given way to other metals: brass, nickel silver, aluminium and then stainless steel, whose cycle of development is still running its course. Yet during this period neither the type nor the nature of the objets themselves have changed, and my town remains dominated by this industrial specialization. Along the shores of Lake San Giulio, amongst the Romanesque churches and the Baroque chapels, the household goods factories have become a precise point of reference, leaving their strong social and cultural imprint on the whole area. One of those early craftsmen/small businessmen was my grandfather, Giovanni Alessi. This book sets out to tell the tale of how a deep-rooted, hard, traditional and perhaps even inward-looking manufacturing tradition has blossomed into our own business venture, on the contrary characterized by constant innovation, open to experimentation and to the paradoxical results of casting from a poetic mould. How Alessi has changed from being a "Workshop for the working of brass and nickel silver plates, with foundry" (so read the sign over our stand at the first Milan Trade Fairs in the twenties) into one of the "factories of Italian design". The change from a metallurgical and mechanical industry into a workshop actively researching the field of applied arts has been

a gradual one over several decades. It has been an exciting process which, quite possibly, could serve as a possible model for the evolution of many kinds of industry in our consumer society. This too is a reason to read on.

▲ The *Omegna Tablet in Orthographic Characters*, designed by Luigi Serafini in 1985, is a wry, pseudo-archaeological look at the "meaning" of Alessi and its history.

The 1920s and 1930s

▲ FAO, or Fratelli Alessi Omegna: the overlapping letters of the first historic logo with vaguely deco curves.

▼ Company founder Giovanni Alessi began as a particularly skilful maker of brass knobs.

● Grandpa Giovanni was a talented sheet-metal worker. In 1921 he bought a plot of land at Omegna and founded Alessi. He started handmaking objects for the table and for the home in copper, brass and nickel silver, which where then either nickel-, chrome- or silver-plated. Grandpa was a real stickler for quality and for work well done: the things he made quickly won acclaim for their workmanship and perfect finish.

▲ Something of an epicure, Grandpa came away from long meals with inspiration for new objects. Here he is with his friend "Cichin" Lagostina.

▶ An engraving of the old factory at Crusinallo, set in the Alpine foothills. Today the scene looks like an industrial archaeological landscape.

◄ The first items produced by Alessi were inspired by the canons dictated by the most famous household goods companies at the start of this century, particularly Austrian and English factories. The materials (brass and nickel silver) are typical of household preferences during the twenties.

▲ Alessi in the early days: the cleaning department. Items were manufactured to order, according to the specific requirements of the customer —a way of working still based on a crafts approach.

▲ Engravings in the early catalogues are a time machine back to middle-class tastes of the day.

▶ An interesting example of a typical—now extinct—object on Italian tables between the two wars: a *Flask holder* (1925).

▼ Double services (teapot, coffee pot, sugar bowl and milk jug on a tray) are the mainstay of output.

ALESSI

▶ Starting in 1924 the
Fratelli Alessi Omegna
company began
manufacturing coffee pots
and trays, as well as small
household items.
Still no pots and pans or
cutlery, items requiring
more complex materials
and processing.

▲ The illustrations on these
pages are based upon some
of the objects found in the
oldest Alessi catalogues, as
reinterpreted by air-brush
artist Tiger Tateishi in 1979.

▶ The quality of Giovanni Alessi's household articles improved rapidly, thanks to technical innovations such as chroming by galvanic bath, nickel-plating and silver-plating. These objects had the no-nonsense solidity of everyday common sense, finished with delicate and traditional ornamental elements.

◀ As Alessandro Mendini points out in his 1979 book *Paesaggio casalingo*, until the thirties developments within the company took the form of an analytical building up of standard objects. The catalogues (the earliest of which dates back to 1925) mark the start of an autonomous activity, showing a dense succession of crafted articles for coffee and tea, for the table, bars, and kitchens, corresponding to a highly polite and archaic way of eating. Objects of this kind are important more for sociological than aesthetic reasons; they have entered our collective past and our collective memory.

Carlo Alessi

◀ The ALessi FRAtelli eagle
brand logo took flight in
1947, replacing the old FAO
acronym; it was to stay in use
until 1967, when it gave way
to the Cesellleria Alessi brand.

◀ The *Octagonal
tea and coffee service*
was a de rigeur presence
in the possessions of a
"proper family" (1935).

● Design, as we understand
the word today, first made
its appearance with my
father, Carlo. Trained
as an industrial designer
in Novara, he joined the
company when still very
young, dedicating himself
to design right from the
start. He was responsible
for most of the objects
made between the mid-
thirties and 1945, the year
he launched his last project,
that archetype of early
Italian design, the *Bombé*
tea and coffee sets.
In the fifties he took over
from Grandpa at the helm
of the company, completely
giving up (I have never
understood why…) design.

▲ In the fifties my father (here strolling with Leo Oggioni, our first agent for Italy) transformed Alessi from a small business to a true industrial concern, dynamically expanding exports to encompass over sixty countries.

★ **1954** ★

ACCIAIO INOX 18/8

During the war years, as the household goods market slowed down, Alessi produced stars for uniforms and mechanical parts for Savoia Marchetti aeroplanes. After the war, faced with an enormous demand for brass ladles for the U.S. army, my father doubled the number of machine tools, expanded the company and started mass-production. As he had realized so early, stainless steel was set to conquer the space vacated by chromed metals and silver-plated alloys.

◀ An overhead view of the *Oil cruet* and *Cheese cellar*, two 1949 prototypes which were initial experiments into a new alloy with a great future ahead of it: stainless steel.

ALESSI

The 1950s and 1960s

▼Carrying on from the preceding decades under Ettore Alessi's technical guidance, the major push into the catering market: the handles and spouts in the *Dani* service (1963) are longer and more pronounced, as if to mirror the personality of objects which though practical are certainly not anonymous; the range includes coffee jugs and cream jugs.

● Uncle Ettore, eleven years younger than his brother, joined my father in 1945. Although he no longer officially works for the company, he remains the great authority on cold pressing of metals. I affectionately refer to him as our "mega-technical director". As head of the technical department, in 1955 he opened Alessi up to collaboration with external designers; working with architects Carlo Mazzeri, Luigi Massoni and Anselmo Vitale the result was several ranges of objects, particularly for the catering trade, many of which are still big sellers.

▲ The wire *Citrus basket*, in production from 1952, is a veritable "industrial standard"; it symbolizes our fifties output.

▲ The community service designed around the *101* coffee pot, in production since 1956, numbers twenty-eight different objects, and is the most professional and most popular line in the company's history.

▼ Ettore Alessi strengthened the design identity of the company's technical office, paving the way for development of several best-selling products such as the range of wire *Baskets* and *Fruit bowls.* He oversaw a radical new shift in materials: brass and nickel silver made way for stainless steel, the new king of the household, first brought experimentally to Alessi by Carlo in the late thirties.

▲ The introduction of stainless steel processing brought a number of structural and technical changes to the company.

▲ A project approach means blending the artistic freedom of the designer with the concrete requirements of manufacturing. Inevitably, some ideas are destined not to progress beyond the design stage, such as this double *Sauce-boat* designed by Joe Colombo and Ambrogio Pozzi.

▼ Massoni and Mazzeri's objects are part of *Programme 4*, a cultural shift which introduced the concepts of "designer", "project" and indeed "design" to the world of household articles.

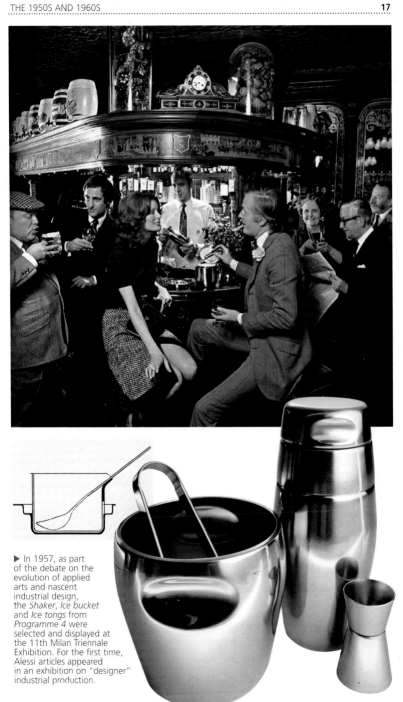

▶ In 1957, as part
of the debate on the
evolution of applied
arts and nascent
industrial design,
the *Shaker, Ice bucket*
and *Ice tongs* from
Programme 4 were
selected and displayed at
the 11th Milan Triennale
Exhibition. For the first time,
Alessi articles appeared
in an exhibition on "designer"
industrial production.

ALESSI

18

▶ The *Avio* (1961) series
includes the tray pictured
below. The name is not only
a tip of the hat to airline
companies, it is a homage
to Alessi's history: mass
manufacture in the 1950s
was only possible because
of supplies from aeronautics
parts suppliers during the
Second World War.

▼ In this "pre-'68"
advertisement the Eiffel Tower
is a rather ingenuous, but
nevertheless explicit, signifier:
internationality and class.
Alessi steel articles gleam on
a swish terrace, counterpoised
perhaps involuntarily, but
most certainly effectively,
against the most spectacular
modern symbol of metal use.

The 1970s

● Officially my career at Alessi began in July 1970, the day after I graduated in law. My dad immediately set me to work on new projects. I threw myself into the job. With a strongly utopian view of "multiplied art", I developed my own brand of cultural-theoretic manifesto championing a new commercial civilization offering the consuming masses veritable artistic items at low prices.

▲ The designers signed up for the "art multiples" were Italian sculptors Giò Pomodoro, Carmelo Cappello, Pietro Consagra and Andrea Cascella, with Yugoslav Dušan Džamonja. The process was a kind of collective madness which tied up our mechanical workshop for almost three years. Staring at the Salvador Dalí prototype my father decided the moment had come to pull the plug on the escapade: but I had already bought the 50,000 steel hooks to manufacture the first 1000 multiples.

◀ Franco Sargiani and Eija Helander are the first designers I brought to Alessi. The partnership with them extended to graphic design, packaging and stand design, as well as the Crusinallo offices. Attempting to rationalize fundamental aspects of corporate life was a huge job. The new *Alessi* logotype began to be used in 1971.

▲ Here the Alessi stands designed by the Sargiani-Helander duo in the early seventies.

▲ The company offices at Crusinallo are also a Franco Sargiani collaboration.

▶ My brother Michele's home at Suna (1981) is, in my opinion, one of the best projects Franco has done for us.

▼ A strong bond grew with
the extrovert and enthusiastic
Franco. Development of
Programme 8 took five years.
The basic idea: total component
mobility of basically square or
rectangular objects, which were
difficult to manufacture in steel.
A true international innovation
in household objects in the
seventies, it was backed up by
a major advertising campaign.

◀ In 1972 Sargiani accepted the request to introduce me to some top designers to launch *Programme 7*. The first contacts were with the Milan-based Exhibition design group. Under the leadership of Silvio Coppola (left), Pino Tovaglia, Franco Grignani, Giulio Confalonieri and Bruno Munari all worked for us, though the resulting designs didn't ever see the light of day. With hindsight, I recognize that those objects still belonged to 1960s style "Bel design Italiano".

▲ The *Tiffany* tray (1974–97) symbolized the range: 10,000 items per year, and a turnover which cheered the intolerant and ferocious Coppola. Sales this big were of huge importance to me: I had proved that designer items could sell well! It was around that time that Dad started going fishing every Thursday.

◀ Coppola's baskets and trays combine tightly packed graphic analysis complete with minuscule handwritten notes, and an innovative use of technological research. His work focused on finding new ways to perforate and shape steel sheeting, wire and gratings. This series had a tough genesis, particularly because of how complex it was to mount the objects, but the public response was extremely encouraging: Tovaglia's *Teorema* tray (1973, out of production), Confalonieri's *Maya* basket (1977) and Coppola's *Square* basket (1977) provided us with a balanced and in its own way classic form of high quality "modern" which was by no means too extravagant.

Ettore Sottsass

● Ettore Sottsass came to Crusinallo in 1972, on Sargiani's invitation. Uncle Ettore and I met him; I was really impressed. He was preceded by the fame of his work for Olivetti, his reputation as the guru of radical design... and he was the first person of truly international standing with whom I had dealings. He is something of a philosopher, bursting with charisma, and he has something interesting to say about everything. It was with him that I began talking over the "high" topics of design, the role of industry in society. Although we meet up only once in a while— due to a certain shyness on my part, as if I was afraid of using up the relationship with him— he was the first person I met through work who for me has become a real mentor, one of my maestros.

▶ One truly unique range: the professional articles for the bar and for serving wine, designed by Sottsass in 1979 with assistance from Alberto Gozzi, taking a cue from the perfect cocktails prepared with such expertise by David Niven in those fifties movies.

▼ The range takes its name from the American shaker (Boston), and includes the *Wine cooler* in two versions (for Bordeaux style or for magnums), supplied— if requested—with a special *Stand*, *Strainer*, *Ice tongs* and *Stirrer*.

▶ A homage to Gauguin intimated in this ad conveys the impression that Sottsass's *Holder and oven-to-table porcelain dish* is an instant classic: technical and stylistic details in common with the *5070* condiment set.

▼ Sottsass does not discriminate between materials: he is one of the most prolific designers in wood, as in his late eighties Twergi line.

▼ The *Tray*, or to be precise the rectangular "fancy tray" (1982) is a subtle Sottsass jibe at Alessi; he well knows how challenging it is to manufacture stainless steel in boxy shapes.

Design Ettore Sottsass, 1994

eto portapirofila · Holder and oven-to-table dish · Support et plat rzellanschale mit Gestell · Conjunto porta-fuente con fuente

◀ The first items Sottsass designed for Alessi were large, wide-rimmed trays: we quickly decided that was not the right direction, and we asked him to tackle oil cruets. With his Finnish assistant Ulla Salovaara he soon came up with the *5070* condiment set (1978), one of our best designs of the last twenty years, and certainly one of our articles that comes closest to being an "industrial standard". Despite being relatively expensive, this little table-top mosque is our best-selling steel condiment set.

▲*La Bella Tavola* porcelain service saw the light of day in 1993. Sottsass designed this in pure white lines, or in a version with subtle, classic, overlapping blue lines.

▶ His curiosity piqued by the idea, and by the broad spaces left on the ornamental edges, Alighiero Boetti, one of Italy's most original contemporary artists, came up with an elaborate decoration unique in its use of a plethora of shapes and colours.

▲ Ettore has the greatest
number of designs in our
catalogue. His wish, shared by
Alessi, is over time to build up
a complete family of objects
for the table and the kitchen,
as did Josef Hoffmann for
Wiener Werkstätte.

▶ Sottsass also designed
Alessi's Milan showroom
(1987).

▲ The *Ginevra* range of crystal glasses is dedicated to the pleasures of "fine drinking". As well as glasses and goblets of varying sizes, there is also a *Decanter*, so beloved of the connoisseur.

▼ Designed in 1987, with the assistance of Alberto Gozzi, the *Nuovo Milano* cutlery set has become a classic, winning the XVIth Compasso d'oro award.

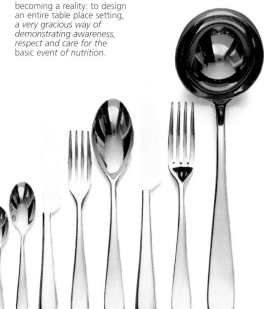

▲ Sottsass's ambition is becoming a reality: to design an entire table place setting, *a very gracious way of demonstrating awareness, respect and care for the* basic *event of nutrition*.

▼ For many years I had wanted to tackle very basic objects, such as these *Castors* (for sugar, salt, cocoa powder, cheese, pepper, chili pepper etc.) and *Butter dishes*, inspired by the static nature of the pictures of American painter Edward Hopper. Ettore did things his own way, forsaking glass for PMMA covered in delicate see-through hues through which the contents may be glimpsed (1998).

▶ The big *Sugar bowl* and spoon, in steel and plastic, is also from 1998.

▼ In the flood of objects Sottsass has designed for Alessi, rare have been his forays into the coffee world: but in the shadow of the smoking totem of a coffee pot (not his, because we don't have any of his in production as yet, but there's still Sapper, Rossi, Graves, Dalisi or King-Kong...), here is his *Sugar and cream set*, with a tray, a blue sugar bowl plus sugar spoon, and a white cream jug (1998).

Richard Sapper

" No, the Japanese are not a threat; they don't have garages… "

● Richard first came to Crusinallo on Shrove Tuesday, 1977. Ettore Sottsass recommended him in these terms: *He's the Tizio lamp guy, the guy who has never done a bad design.* Dad, Uncle Ettore and I greeted him. He was dressed all in black and wearing a bizarre piper's hat. Sapper usually works on just a few designs at a time, only things that really interest him; it's hard to force him into a narrow brief: far better to give him free reign, at a rate of roughly one new project every five years.

▲ Sapper has designed some items which have become historic not just in design terms, but also for Alessi's economic fortunes: the *9090* coffee pot (next page, above). Launched in 1979, this was Alessi's first project for the kitchen; until then we had focused only on objects for the dining and living room.

ALESSI

▲ Two flagship Sapper designs for Alessi: coffee pot *9090* (the first coffee pot manufactured at Crusinallo, awarded the XIth Compasso d'oro and on display at the MoMA in New York), and the majestic *Kettle with a singing whistle*, inspired by the sound of the steamers and barges that ply the Rhine, the first "designer" kettle (1982).

◄ The *Kettle* is characterized by two pitch-pipes in "E" and "B" lodged in the brass whistle pipes. Small devices commonly used to tune musical instruments, they are specially made for us by craftsmen in the Black Forest.

Alberto Gozzi (in the picture with glasses), an expert gourmet, and teacher of advanced courses for catering school teachers, has worked as a gastronomical advisor on many Alessi projects.

A few years ago he was "pinched" by the Italian President, who summoned him to Rome to run the catering at the Quirinale Palace. A richly deserved promotion.

▶ A real thorn in the side of our engineers, Sapper's presence in the company has to be carefully regulated to prevent sparks flying. In the best Ulm school tradition— "the designer must, by definition, know the technology he works with intimately"—Sapper considers himself an expert on every manufacturing topic: because of the countless hard-to-make details in his designs, he gets into long and hotly contested arguments with the engineers. The results are stunning: the *Bandung* "automatic" tea maker, (1995, below) and his most recent project, the *Cobán* electric coffee maker, which aroused the same feelings in me when I saw its earliest prototype as the *9090* coffee pot did, sixteen years ago.

NESPRESSO

▲ The *Cobán* (1997) was launched in four versions to cater to the personal tastes of vast numbers of coffee drinkers. The two traditional versions (with and without coffee grinder) are joined by two innovative ones using pre-packed easy-to-use coffee doses: the *Nespresso*, which uses proprietary coffee portion doses, and the *Easy Serving Espresso*, which takes E.S.E. single use coffee portions (both 1998).

ALESSI

34

Sapper is also the man behind the most complex project I have ever worked on: the *Cintura di Orione* range of cooking utensils, made possible thanks to Professor Alberto Gozzi's fundamental help and designed to accommodate the suggestions of several famous French and Italian chefs and experts in European cookery. The research project, begun in 1979—now available in a historical volume—was dedicated to a group that, until then, had been somewhat neglected by the market: "private gourmets", people with a passion for inventive and creative cookery.

▶ **Roger Vergé**

Blending innovation and tradition, he finished off the unusual large oval-shaped *Fish poacher with rack* (60 centimetres long), ideal for cooking fish of varying sizes, as well as pig's trotters.

◀ **Thuilier & Charial**

The godfather of French cuisine was a consultant on the *Oval casserole*, a cast iron pot ideal for slow cooking stews and braised meats. The strong material and heavy lid keep in all the steam and flavours.

▶ **Pierre and Michel Troisgros**

The Lyon-based masters in Nouvelle Cuisine
worked on the *Black-iron frying pans* (curves
specially designed to facilitate omelet flip
acrobatics), the *Long-handled saucepan*,
and the delightful single-serving *Cassolette*.

▼ **Gualtiero Marchesi**

The Italian "creative chef"
par excellence worked on the
more traditional items, such
as the *Stockpot* and the two
copper and steel *Casseroles*.

◀ Angelo Paracucchi

A great exponent of Mediterranean cooking, worked with Sapper on the *Flambé pan* and *Lamp*, objects right out of the spectacular traditions of the Belle Époque, re-invented in a modern interpretation.

▶ Alain Chapel

The undisputed international authority on sauces worked on the copper and steel *Sauteuse* with flared sides, adding a *Whisk* for beating and mixing.

Achille Castiglioni

" *Naturally, Alessi design concept is so broad that there was just the right space and positioning for my own design concept. And I feel great in this space… this element of enjoyment is an integral part of both my own and Alessi's design.* "

● I clearly remember the first time I met this great legend of Italian design, Castiglioni, in his Milan studio at Piazza Castello: we soon worked out a possible area of collaboration, the *Dry* service range of cutlery. I consider Castiglioni a great master, a man of insatiable curiosity, blessed with great irony and exceptional modesty; a man who can design masterpieces. He is very realistic, like the good Milanese gent he is, and he understands his audience well. The best way to get him to work is to bring him an idea that tickles him. Our best ideas have come to us late in the evening, over a tumbler of whisky.

▶ The three Castiglioni brothers in sporting garb, in a drawing/caricature from the thirties.

▼The *Fruit bowl-colander*
(1995) responds to two
fundamentals for Castiglioni:
providing a practical solution
to small "dining at table"
problems, where possible
with a small but intelligent
functional innovation, plus
the people's preference
for a polished metal finish.
In a broad Milanese accent,
Castiglioni sums up:
cinc ghèi pussée, ma luster
(*five lire more, but shiny*).

◀To solve the *Ash-tray*
conundrum—torment and
delight of many a designer—
Castiglioni, an absent-minded
smoker, provides an ingenious
solution: a spiral spring (easy to
extract for cleaning) holds the
cigarette and prevents it from
falling (1970).

▲ Over thirty years separate the two designs in this photo, both manufactured in 1996: the *Ondula* fruit bowl and *Firenze* wall clock, designed with his brother Pier Giacomo for the 1965 "La casa abitata" exhibition held at Palazzo Strozzi, Florence.

▲ *Wristwatch*, created with the graphic input of Max Huber for the dial, in production between 1988 and 1993.

▶ *Foldable tray*, with retractable sections to vary its dimensions, never went into production (1982).

ALESSI

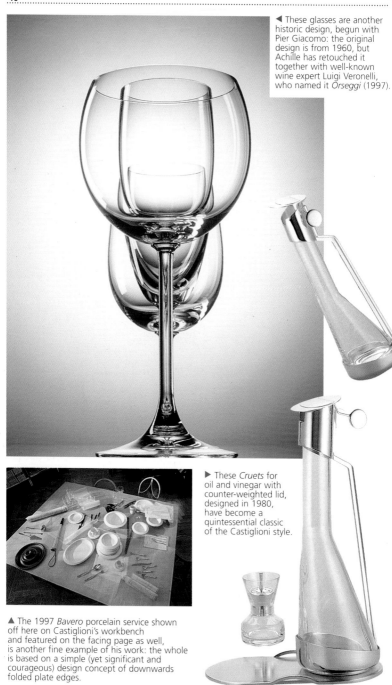

◄ These glasses are another historic design, begun with Pier Giacomo: the original design is from 1960, but Achille has retouched it together with well-known wine expert Luigi Veronelli, who named it *Ôrseggi* (1997).

▶ These *Cruets* for oil and vinegar with counter-weighted lid, designed in 1980, have become a quintessential classic of the Castiglioni style.

▲ The 1997 *Bavero* porcelain service shown off here on Castiglioni's workbench and featured on the facing page as well, is another fine example of his work: the whole is based on a simple (yet significant and courageous) design concept of downwards folded plate edges.

▲ The *Grand Prix* cutlery set won first prize in the competition held by Gio Ponti for Reed & Barton in 1960, but never produced, probably because of the extreme technical complexity of making the knife. The set has been included in the catalogue since 1997.

▼ The *Dry* service marked our debut in cutlery manufacture (1982).

▶ Picking up on the theme of *ready-made*, this prototype seven-armed candelabra is called *Menorah*, and rests on the rubber covering of a Japanese motorbike grip. Three of them were produced for the "Nerot Mitzvah, Contemporary ideas for light in the Jewish Ritual" research project, promoted by our common friend Izzika Gaon of the Israel Museum in Jerusalem.

◀ Castiglioni's sense of practicality, his attention to everyday whims, come out in the *Mayonnaise spoon*, conceived specially for scooping up the stuff that sticks to the inside of the jar. This spoon was originally designed with Pier Giacomo as a promotional gadget for Kraft, and manufactured by us in 1997.

Alessandro Mendini

BOOK

PAESAGGIO CASALINGO

● It is by no means easy to describe Alessandro Mendini's relations with myself and Alessi. What I can say is that for me he has been the master, in a vaguely Socratic fashion, who has gradually introduced me to the many mysteries of our fascinating profession. When people ask me what Mendini does for us, what his role is, I can only smile: Sandro is such a *sui generis* consultant that his position cannot really be described outside its context: a relationship similar to Peter Behrens' with AEG of Rathenau.

Mendini began working with us in 1977 when, under his guidance, a design and architecture magazine destined to make quite a stir over the following years, *Modo*, first started.

▲ It is Mendini who designed my living space, the "House of Happiness." As well as drawing the plan (above), Alessandro coordinated the work of the other architects involved.

▶ The series of small kitchen electrical tools saw Mendini right in the midst of a joint venture uniting Alessi and Philips, opening up new horizons for international partnerships.

▲ Typical of Mendini's work are the meticulous "maps" in which characters, objects, things and settings are placed in a chain of relations, as in a topographical sequence, in which every step adds to understanding the meaning of the journey.

ALESSANDRO MENDINI

▶ Somehow, in an extremely informal way, Mendini is aware of our most intimate problems and wishes… without even meeting up that often; over the years we have perfected a way of working together that is almost telepathic…

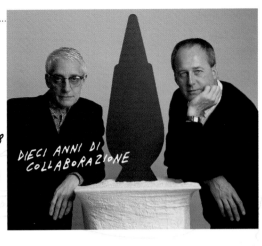

1988

A·ALESSI
A·MENDINI

CENTRO STUDI — LAURA

DIECI ANNI DI COLLABORAZIONE

▼ *Recinto* is a rectangular tray with scalloped edges available in blue and orange (1998). Once again Mendini comes to the rescue of the absent-minded and clumsy. This tremble-proof tray comes with wide handles for good grip and a "safety" margin: even in its form, the tray's profile hints at handing out generous servings, not without a touch of self-irony.

SERVIZIO PIATTI

◀ In 1986 a porcelain plate service designed by Mendini, assisted by Annalisa Margarini, went into production. Alessandro came up with the basic service, in white, and the *How many stars* version, with delicate gilded ornaments, while the polychrome triangles in the very vivacious *How many colours* decoration are by Nicola De Maria.

TRAY

ALESSI

Author of the research project *Paesaggio casalingo* and other books, Mendini is Alessi's official chronicler. As a designer, he continues to design objects, often in the most complex and moving areas of our catalogue. As an architect, he has designed my home (the "House of Happiness"), two extensions for the factory at Crusinallo, the Alessi museum and the layout of several exhibitions. In his role as design manager he has been responsible for the invention and coordination of some of our most legendary design processes, a few of which are illustrated here.

As a consultant, he has brought to my attention a huge number of designers who have gone on to work with us.

◀ I'm especially proud of the *Anna G.* corkscrew (1994), which immediately became our top bestseller, thereby debunking the rumour (slyly put about by the man himself) that Mendini only designs objects which don't sell! After this success, the inevitable little family followed, including a *Timer*, *Candle holder* (1999), *Table cigar lighter*, *Pepper mill*, *Pressure* and *Wine caps*, and *Champagne cap* (1998).

◀ The Atelier Mendini designed the decor and image of Alessi shops in various cities around the world; their work melds together a fairytale element with something of the *Wunderkammer*, the "chamber of wonders" so popular among Renaissance and Baroque collectors. The display areas have the unenviable task of encapsulating the idea of the "dream factory", and taking visitors on an adventure in design as they journey through our household landscape. More than 100 designers, 20 "families", 600 designs and 250 new items every year, a veritable encyclopaedia, inviting us to leaf through its pages.

▲ For the Alessi building in Tokyo (1999) the Atelier Mendini has built upon DNA very similar to that of the Crusinallo factory, establishing a "family feeling" that spans continents. The same thing is true of Oslo and Helsinki (1998); a specific architecture and design approach, as we seek to be recognized as creators of one of the major chain store concepts in the history of architecture.

ALESSI

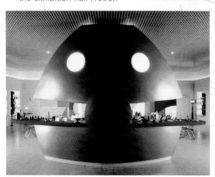

▲ Alessi's Crusinallo headquarters (1994) bears the mark of the Atelier Mendini, with a vital contribution by Francesco Mendini: here, the plan for extension, and the polychrome stairs leading from the reception area to the exhibition hall (1995).

◄ The allusive Alessi stand at the Frankfurt Fair.

◀ The Omegna *Forum*, the new museum of local arts and traditions (1998), designed by the Atelier Mendini.

▼ The headquarters of the Omegna Volontari del Soccorso (in actual fact located in the Crusinallo area) was also opened in 1998.

◀ The conference room at Alessi's Hamburg offices, a Mendini design too, with the reassuring shapes of the *100% Make up* vases (1996).

▶ The interior of the first Macef stand, with its characteristic revolving display area.

Tea & Coffee Piazza

▲ Robert Venturi's objects, marked by their subtle decoration, are set on a tray reproducing Piazza Campidoglio.

● In 1979 Alessandro Mendini's exuberant mind came up with the idea of setting "pure" architects the task of designing an object, the classic tea and coffee service. Produced in a run of ninety-nine each, the eleven silver services came out with the Officina Alessi brand and the designer's monogram. In 1983 they were presented to the public in an exhibition arranged by Hans Hollein at the San Carpoforo church in Milan.

▲ Japanese logic and precision for Kazumasa Yamashita: the knobs of these recipients form the initials of their contents.

◄ Ironic and eclectic postmodern for Charles Jencks, who designs extravagant tubby columns with capitals, somewhere between surprise and parody.

▶ With this project Aldo Rossi demonstrates his talents as a designer: the tray turns into a home tabernacle to officiate the hospitable rite of coffee.

▼ Paolo Portoghesi uses hexagons and pyramids to sculpt a domestic citadel for those little pleasures, even—the only designer to do so—adding an ash-tray for smokers.

▼ It's all curves in Alessandro Mendini's design, which seems to breathe new life into the timeless *Bombé*: the articles are ready to leap from their slender pedestals.

ALESSI

◀ Viewed from above, Michael Graves's objects recall the outline of biscuits, expressing their convivial appearance in the refined materials.

▼ Óscar Tusquets's objects consist of two soldered shells with riveting in relief along an oblique axis.

▼ Hans Hollein fits his items along one side of a tray recalling the bridge of an aircraft carrier; Hollein also designed the "wall" for displaying the eleven services.

▼ Eerie little hands poke out of Stanley Tigerman's tray, while the spouts are shaped as inviting half-open lips (a detail requiring a high-risk technical approach).

The *Tea & Coffee Piazza* series takes up and develops two major themes: the concept of "artistic multiple" and the involvement of international architects in the quest for design. This feature was strongly promoted by Mendini, who foretold the end of "Bel design italiano" and, setting himself "at the crossroads between awareness of tradition and the lure of the unknown", felt the need to go back to the roots of the phenomenon of design,

to the fifties, when "pure" architects began to design objects. Indeed, not only did this venture start off the trend of highly expressive, postmodern "objects of emotion" *style symbol*, it enabled me to make an incredible number of contacts and have new experiences which would come in very handy for the product policy of the following years. As a research venture, we owe it the discovery of two great new designers: Aldo Rossi and Michael Graves.

▼ Richard Meier studied a complex integration of square volumes and rounded forms, in a brilliant play of inside and outside, container and contents.

ALESSI

Aldo Rossi

●Aldo Rossi was a lake-lover like me. He was never happier than when he went to meditate and write at the old family house on Lake Mergozzo, I found out when we first met in the spring of 1980. He designed some of the most representative of our eighties articles, and had an ability—which only the great designers have—to tune in to the public mood. Rossi regarded design as something of a hobby; his first love was always architecture. He died in an accident on Lake Maggiore. The first of my masters to pass away. I miss him terribly, I'm very sad to say.

" *I feel there is often something mysterious in the process of selling objects: sometimes I see objects as clay relics ranged in museums; a material enclosing a world that perhaps merely desires to be used and destroyed. There are always two ways of looking at things…* "

▶ The *Momento* range of watches (1987) is the only one still in the Alessi catalogue. Aldo loved watches and clocks, often incorporating them into his public buildings.

◀ Rossi's dream was to produce a new Moka to sell to all, if possible at a low price: he got very close with his *La cupola* aluminium espresso coffee maker (1988).

◀ Throughout August 1997 I kept the prototype of his *Pitcher* in my car: I knew that Aldo was due to come to Lake Maggiore, and he would have been happy to see it. He never got the chance.

▼ The *Press filter coffee maker* made during the research that resulted in *Cupola* (1986).

As can be seen from the design of a coffee-maker "protected" by *San Carlone* of Arona, Aldo had a way of relating to our engineers that was worlds away from what we had experienced: he made sketches, presented them, and then waited for the engineers to make all their comments and changes, even sweeping ones.

It seemed as if everything was OK! For Uncle and Casalino, fresh from the relationship with Sapper, this was a scandalous attitude. One day Uncle said to him in his grumpy way:

But, really, couldn't you bring us finished designs rather than these sketches which are only half done?

That was the only time I ever saw Rossi get angry. He answered dryly that if we wanted final-draft technical designs, then we could get them from Zanuso, but not from him. Rossi's attitude helped me to understand an approach to design not restricted to himself, but shared to some degree by all or almost all designers who have experience as architects.

ALESSI

il ritorno dalla scu...

▲ The book *La conica e altre caffettiere* (1984) is the result of his research into the making and serving of coffee.

◄ Rossi's designs always reveal an (often playful, always explanatory) relationship between the design object and constructive architecture.

▶ *La cubica*, in cast aluminium, is Aldo's homage to the saying *Form follows function*: it is the ideal utensil for cooking cubic tomatoes. Because of the great technical challenges and the high production costs, only a few hundred have been made, starting in 1991.

▶ *La conica*, which Rossi designed between 1980 and 1983, started life as an evolution of Aldo's contribution to the *Tea & Coffee Piazza* project, translating a precious silver object into a mass-produceable steel product, with the new attributes of solidity and ease-of-use. Initially Rossi was a little wary of industry in general, but he liked Alessi and he threw himself into long research projects regarding coffee-related items, which were to become a kind of obsession for him: notes, sketches, photographs, designs, multifarious projects such as the percolator, the *New Orleans* model for American-style coffee... For Rossi the coffee maker (finally produced in two versions, *conical* and *domed*, from 1984) perfectly symbolized the dialectic relation between architecture (better still, town planning) and the "household landscape" into which this miniature monument fits.

▼ Beyond coffee makers, Rossi's work for Alessi is eclectic to say the least, spanning wristwatches and wall clocks to the tower-belvedere designed for the "House of Happiness", yet to be built and here shown in photo-montage.

▼ Rossi started out from a formal and expressive "strong idea", capable of resisting all the modifications required by the engineers. *You know far better than I how to make a coffee maker*, Aldo said to a speechless Casalino. This attitude of delegating the manufacturing details is why it is much easier and more relaxing for our engineers to work with architects rather than designers.

ALESSI

In the days of the "famous" clash over technical drawings, my uncle was bewildered, but at the next opportunity he managed to redeem himself by comparing Aldo's designs to those of Morandi. Aldo was struck, and from that moment a great passion grew between the two of them, culminating in the design for my cousin Stefano's house at Suna (1995).

Michael Graves

" With Alessi, tradition extends to the idea of family. As a designer you and your people are brought in and treated as a member of a family—it's a very personal relationship of designer and manufacturer. This is what ties everything. "

● As far back as January 1980, during our first visit to his big studio in Princeton, Michael Graves told us that from then on he would be spending at least half his time on design. It was a definitive statement, one which corresponded to his great potential. He has an incredible ability to tune in to public taste, even that of the man on the street: he is not a lover of theory, but he once admitted his wish to help create an "American style".

▶ The 1985 *Kettle with bird* continues to go from strength to strength. It spawned a "family" of objects which Graves dauntlessly continues to expand, year after year, developing his own sensitivity towards a less intellectualized approach to design, softer than its European equivalents.

ALESSI

Graves's highly personal and easy to recognize formal style blends influences from the European tradition, Art Deco, American "pop", and flashes of pre-Columbian culture. He has shown he can bewitch the public like only very few of the designers with whom I've worked. I think that his success derives from his wholly uninhibited approach to the economic dimension which this activity inevitably entails, an attitude that enables him to read the expectations of the public more clearly than his European counterparts.

▶ The articles in the "Graves family" came to life concentrically, developing around the Kettle, which was initially joined by the Cream jug, the Sugar bowl (1988) and the big two-litre Carafe (1991). Reinforcements arrived in the shape of Pelican (1995), the espresso coffee maker. Graves has made multiple versions of many objects, for example his Oil cruets (1994).

▲ The designs in the background are from sketches for the service he made as part of the Tea & Coffee Piazza project, the first time Graves and Alessi worked together.

◄ *Corkscrew, Champagne cap, Pepper mill, Salt castor* and *Kitchen timer*: for Graves the concept of "family" spans a horizon of different items, every year increasing in extent, right down to the tiniest of pieces.

▲ *Demitasse cup, Mug, Butter dish* and *Press filter coffee maker*: an unmistakable look for objects well shielded by rings of steel, with easy-grip handles, ideal for those drowsy, half-asleep breakfasts (1989).

▲ Polyamide handles make a comeback in this indispensable *Tray* (1994), while the *Photo holder* has joined the family (1997).

ALESSI

▶ With its characteristic shape *Medium* vase (1997) looks a little like a porcelain rendition of cut bamboo, a paradoxical and worthy citation of vases made in Malaysia, the only country in the world not to use ceramics.

▼ The *Kitchen clock* is the missing link between the "birdie" family (the bird is on the hands) and the bright colours of the *Euclid* series (1992).

▶ As well as his wooden objects for *Twergi*, Graves miniaturized architecture for this *Mantel clock*, with the clock face on the "piano nobile" of an edifice supported by squat columns (1988).

◀ The *Bread bin* (1997) takes us back to a special spot in Graves's memory: the paunchy recipient is replete with nostalgia for the breakfast American children used to eat before the ready-made snack age, when it was an indispensable treasure chest guarding the aroma of freshly baked bread.

▼ The delicate colour combination of yellow and blue sets off one of Graves's two *Porcelain services*.

▶ The *Cheese board* rests on a broad steel tray, and is made up of a ceramic cutting board "with holes", crowned by a transparent cover: the handle is a smiling mouse. Available in a range of colours, as is the *Bread bin* above.

ALESSI

▼ With its reassuring rotundities, solidly placed on cubic bases, the *Jug with vacuum glass* (1994) has become the symbol of the *Euclid* series: available colours include a "Graves blue".

▲ These porcelain *Trivets* bear the silhouette of the *Kettle with bird*: the four colours (cobalt blue, celadon green, white and melba yellow) match those of the vase and candle holders.

▲ In his most recent work for Alessi, Graves has focused on porcelain, transferring typically architectural motifs to objects which could be considered the "skyscrapers" of the table top: *Candlestick* and the *Vase* (26 centimetres tall) decorated with an ivory-coloured medallion.

Other Designers

● I have worked with hundreds of designers since the early seventies. This has been the most rewarding experience of my life, and I continue to be thrilled by it. I am a lucky man: each of these encounters has left me with something of importance. I love seeing how, each time, the vastness of the Creative Possible gels into images, words, gestures and thoughts, always unique, yet always focused on the heroic exploit of expressing something that is larger than we are. I am yet to understand the mysterious way that some of these designers have built up families in our catalogue, while many others have seemingly left a more fleeting trace… But what I do know is that just one project is all it takes to add something to this great game of life.

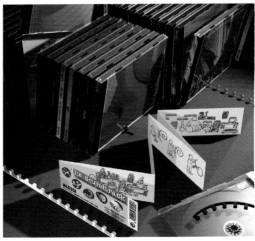

▲ *The Soundtrack* is a new departure for Alessi: a self-adhesive compact disc holder in thermoplastic resin. The decoration is designed by Javier Mariscal. I had been working for many years with Ron, without finding anything for a production run, until one evening in the spring of 1997 he called me, saying he had a great project for me, that he would fax it to me right away. How thrilling! After so many years, for the first time I had before me a concrete example of what I call *Less is more*, the personification of the prophecy of immaterial design for the next century, the absence of an authoritative personal style. And what class! *The Soundtrack* is one of the most brilliant projects I have come across in at least ten years.

▲ *Rosenschale* is the critical reconstruction of the prototype of a fruit basket designed by Josef Hoffmann in 1906, and never manufactured. Arnell and Bickford worked solely from a photograph—no sketches or drawings have ever been found.

ALESSI

Andrea Branzi

Building a house for somebody means building a place and objects with which one can enter in relations, not just of use and functionality, but also psychological, symbolic and poetic. Holderlin used to say Man lives poetically, which means that the relations that link a person to his nest are literary in nature—partly obscure— and symbolic.

▶ *Mama-ò*, Branzi's kettle designed in 1988, has two symmetrical spouts with a melodic whistle, connected by a long handle.

◀ Concerned about ecology and natural forms, Branzi is one of the designers most sensitive to the turned wood of *Twergi*. His family, recognizable by their lengthened, linked lozenge decoration also includes the witty *Toothpick holder* (1991) and the *Bottle-opener* (1999).

▶ Inevitably drawn from Branzi's own life (he has three sisters who married three brothers), is his passion for family trees and for "judicious couplings". Branzi has patiently and diligently collated and illustrated his *Genetic Tales* into a book. With complete lack of modesty he defines it a catalogue *collecting*

(almost) all examples of man alive at this end of the millennium. This research has resulted in a family of objects ranging from the *T-shirt* to the *Mug*. This tall (100 cm) vase is in many ways the patriarch of the *Genetic Tales* line. It is turned by hand in white ceramic with blue decoration, in a limited edition of 99 pieces.

ALESSI

68

Norman Foster

◄ With his rectangular coloured aluminium *Tray* (1998) Foster returns to the smooth and essential simplicity of certain Japanese objects, such as super low futons. Such simplicity in everyday gesture (setting something down, sleeping) is reflected in the pleasing and solid "grip" afforded by the pear wood, while the gentle curve adds a relaxing softness to the tray's shape.

Shigeru Uchida

▶ *Dear Vera* bears the name of Aldo Rossi's daughter: the table clock in two versions was originally designed to furnish the Fukuoka hotel, which Uchida and Rossi designed together (1994–98).

▼ Captivated by the whimsical crumpled effect of a silver paper tray, Clotet reproduced the effect in stainless steel (1994).

Lluís Clotet

Riccardo Dalisi

▶ His research into the *Neapolitan coffee maker* (1979–87, winning the XIIth Compasso d'Oro) was the longest in our history: over the years it led to one book and over two hundred fully working prototypes in tin. Wearing a beret and clothes straight out of a neo-realist film, continuously turning over new ideas and trying out new ways of making things work, Dalisi has not been an easy person to manage, but this was a very important project for us indeed. It enabled us to open up our manufacturing world even more to the conceptual experience of the artisan; it taught us to dilute our certainties in a fragile and poetic light, which is so necessary to work on extremely deep-rooted household rituals.

Jasper Morrison

● What I like about Morrison
is the courage and modesty he
brings to his life as a designer.
He knows only too well that in
our field major innovation
hardly ever comes about from
great leaps forward, but rather
it is the result of small and
progressive improvements,
dominated by the rich and
fertile terrain of ancient ritual.

▲ The *Twin salad bowl*
(1998) is all the more striking
for the simple archetypal
elegance of its form,
produced by the functional
invention of a twin cover, and
for the precision with which
one approaches the gesture
of serving-offering. The small
notch in the edge of the
bowl is designed for a
thumb, to give extra grip, or
as a recess for salad servers.

▶ Casbah, sweet casbah...
Pepe le Moko (1998) grinds
sea salt and various types
of peppercorns..

◄ *Socrates* is a corkscrew
(1998): the philosopher's
maieutics strike again, providing
expression of the ideas within
the person/object with whom
you have a dialogue.

▶ *Tin family* (1998) is a family
of stainless steel containers
for storing salt, sugar, cereals,
biscuits and cakes. Morrison
takes the history of design
types forwards once more,
cautiously and bravely taking
small but crucial steps.

▼ Interactivity, solutions
for two objects which can
be brought together: *Op* is
a tray; *Op-la* turns into
a table-tray with a stainless
steel base (1998).

Massimo Morozzi

◄ *Pasta set* is, simply, a homage to pasta. Morozzi showed me the project in 1982. The shape of the object was attractive and yet mysterious. We organized a survey: roughly half of those interviewed did not realize it was a saucepan for boiling water, and came up with all kinds of interpretations. Nevertheless, we decided to manufacture it, and that was a sound decision. *Pasta set* has become so popular that it has had a profound influence on the market, winning the Gold Medal in 1986 at the Ljubljana Bio 11, and spawning at least a hundred imitators the world over. The project continued with *Vapor set* (1990) designed for steam cooking.

Fig. 13

Frank Gehry

▼ *Pito* is the kettle designed by Gehry, with a mahogany handle and melodic stopper.

66 When the artists and sculptors I know are working, there is always an element of play involved. They experiment, try things out. A slightly naïve and infantile way of doing things, like children playing in a sand box. Scientists work in a similar way. It's like casting away baggage until one is free to follow ideas, rather than seeking to see where one is headed. 99

Paolo Portoghesi

◄ The interwoven chapel arches of Achphat in Armenia and the subtle lines of the Tlemcen mosque in North Africa have inspired this micro-architecture, where Portoghesi's trademark bundle of lines culminates in the magical light of a candle (1988–98).

ALESSI

George Sowden

◀Sowden's typical soft, rounded contours and lively colours on his eight function desktop calculator, *Dauphine* (1997).

▶To soften the invasive finality of a timer's ring, Sowden designed *Alphonse* (1997), an electronic timer which, when the time is up, plays a little tune composed by Steve Piccolo. Which tune it plays depends on the object's colour.

▼These *Jaia* porcelain bowls with lids (1997) are available in white or with decorations by A. Fiorilli, N. du Pasquier and by Sowden himself.

Massimo Scolari

▶ Tools to read and write well
by… as computer mice run
rampant, Scolari (the name
aptly means scholars in Italian!)
in 1998 comes up with a
Pencil in ebonized wood
with a lead-tin alloy tip, and a
Paperknife-bookmark, with two
page-marking ribbons, specially
designed for people who read
books whose pages need
cutting.

Oscar Tusquets

▼ Three thermometers
designed by Tusquets, in
production in 1998: as can
be seen, *Blue Sky*, with its
cloud and thunderbolt,
measures the outside
temperature: *Chily Penguin*
prefers the cold inside
refrigerators; the little devil
Hot Sweet Hot just loves
red-hot ovens.

" *What I love about architecture is its complexity and contradiction. I don't like the incoherence and arbitrary nature of bad architecture, nor the over-elaboration of the picturesque or of expressionism. I love hybrid elements rather than pure ones, the results of compromise rather than cleanliness, the crooked rather than the straight, ambiguity rather than articulation. I prefer richness of meaning to clarity of meaning: I prefer disorder bursting with vitality to obvious single-mindedness: I accept the non sequitur and proclaim duality. But architecture founded on complexity and contradiction requires a special kind of commitment to the whole. It has to pursue the elusive unity of inclusion, as opposed to the facile unity of exclusion. More is not less.* "

▼ Part of the *Tea & Coffee Piazza* project, *The Campidoglio* tray (1985) echoes Michelangelo's paving in Rome's Capitol Square, highlighting its exceptional perspective shift between the circle and ellipse.

▲ *Cuckoo clock* (1988–96) is an amusing challenge for Venturi, coming to grips with a popular genre, very different from *Campidoglio*.

Marco Zanuso

▲ The *Duna* range of cutlery (1995) is our sole
Zanuso project, though I see him as something
of the Daddy of Italian design.
This was designed as a submission to
the 1960 competition held by the U.S. firm
Reed & Burton: I clearly recall him describing
the central element of imagination behind
these items as the "narrow life", that
is the tapering of the end part of the handle,
mirroring the dresses of young ladies
from well-to-do fifties families.

ALESSI

Philippe Starck

" *Alessi sells joy!* "

● Starck began working with me in 1986, on the French design project *Projet Solférino*, organized together with the Centre Pompidou and François Burkhardt. I cannot help thinking of Starck as the *designer terrible* of our decade. He is a living example of my dream: design, real design, is always highly charged with innovation towards the world of manufacturing and trade, bringing results that need no longer be justified solely on a technological or balance sheet level. A true work of design must move people, convey feelings, bring back memories, surprise, transgress… it must make us feel, intensely, that we are living our one single life… in sum, it has to be poetic. Design is one of the most apt poetic forms of expression of our day. And I know that this great visionary still has plenty of surprises up his sleeve, despite his threats to retire!

▲ Starck, "hung" on the hooks of his *Faitoo*. Leader of the renaissance in French design, in this brilliant and daring identity photo cum marketing ploy Starck shows he is quick to share the fate of his objects.

◀ A lover of precision instruments (see the *Coo-coo* radio, 1996, right), Starck is also happy to design more commonplace objects, such as this *Dr. Spoon* ear-cleaner, *Dr. Kiss* toothbrush, *Dr. Kleen* toothpick and *Dr. Cheese* inter-dental brush (1998).

◀ The *Hot Bertaa* kettle (1990-1997) is skewered by its handle-spout. During the design stage, its compact, almost sacred appearance was shrouded in an aura of mysticism: in his preliminary sketches Starck had penned a Latin inscription around its base.

▶ With the *Boaat* (1998) series, a range of kitchen containers with lids and bowls with feet, Starck continues his research into archetypal eating objects, this time drawing inspiration from Japanese cuisine.

ALESSI

◄ Starck's *Wall clock* takes up a favourite motif: he liberates the clock hands from their imprisonment, freeing them to roam through space. The clock is made up only of the two hands and its workings: you tell the time from the shadows on the wall, much like a sundial (1990).

▲ Starck's projects have, in time, assumed the name and appearance of animal presences in the domestic environment: here we have the *Max-le-chinois* colander and the suggestive, mysterious, leggy *Juicy Salif* lemon squeezer both from 1990.

▲ *Faitoo*, "fait-tout", came
out in 1996. In French
it means both "do-it-all"
and saucepan. It is a long bar
to hang in the kitchen, with
hooks for hanging all kinds
of things by their handles
or through special holes.
Everything is visible and
within reach, spelling an
end to those frustrating
"where can it be?" moments
in the kitchen.

FAITOO

by STARCK

ALESSI

▲ *Voilà Voilà*: the tray rushes along on its little green feet (1992).

▲ The *Cake server* looks as solid and manoeuvrable as a bricklayer's trowel (1998).

▲ The unmistakable silhouette of *Mister Meumeu* conceals a parmesan cheese cellar with grater: the horn is, in actual fact, a spoon (1992).

▼ The gleaming surface of the *Centre-piece* is supported by "attendants": barely sketched grey or strange characters redolent of Starck's recent "anthropomorphic" works (1996).

◄ Starck's output
spans precision
mechanisms (such as
the clocks or the radio)
and seemingly everyday
objects, such as the
Dr. Skud fly swatter
which, when moved,
reveals a human face
(1998).

WELCOME

▲ In 1996 we acquired the small Starck and
Patricia company, adding several articles to our
catalogue including the *O'Kelvin* candle-stick
(1989), *Joe Cactus* ash-tray (1990) and *Berta
Youssouf* place-holder (1987).

▲ The chubby, solitary
Dedé mediates on his soft
aluminium rotundities and on
his role as a doorstop (1996).

Dédé
design Philippe Starck, (1994) 1996

ALESSI

Enzo Mari

" *Italian design manufacturers are, in actual fact, metaphors for manufacturers.* "

● Enzo Mari harbours a critical attitude towards our company, despite the fact that it is different from the many others on the international design scene. Without question he is my "master of paranoia": a sort of guardian angel on my shoulder who wags a disapproving finger when I do something he feels I shouldn't! We met in the late seventies, when I wanted to include his *Arran* tray, designed for Danese, in our *Programme 7*—and I succeeded, finally, twenty years later, in 1997. In a conference held in Paris, with his characteristic verbal vehemence, he expressed the concept I have cited above. The words struck me, I made them mine, and the phrase has served as a launchpad for theoretical research into the "Factory of Italian Design". I am delighted he is still working and building up his family in our catalogue. I find his criticisms valuable, every now and then we need him to reset the needle of our compass to North, the direction it should be pointing in, even in mid-storm.

▲ *Ecolo* is Mari's most emblematic project: turning discarded plastic bottles into vases for flowers (1996).

▶ Mari has a green thumb, and many of his projects have a strong ecological connotation. The main reason why he created his *Gardening set* for balconies and allotments was probably for his own passion: it includes a stainless steel and aluminium *Trowel* and a pair of dual-purpose tools: a *Trowel/ress* and a *Rake/repotter* (1999).

▲ As this *Alzatina* table fruit stand (1997) shows, Mari is creating a large family of plastic objects, mostly for the kitchen, along the metaproject line of "new simplicity".

▶ This two tier, three wheeled *Standard* trolley (1989) is one of the furnishing accessories designed and tested at my "House of Happiness".

ALESSI

◄ Kitchen articles in plastic demonstrate Mari's "absolute" conception of industrial production: the quest for archetypes in which outwardly commonplace shapes reveal themselves in the full functionality of daily use.

▼ The *Container for kitchen salt and more* in see-through plastic has much in common with the Danese objects: an innovative touch is the hinge, modelled out of a single element (1999).

▼ Mari's work at Alessi also includes re-interpreting now "classic" items in new materials: a perfect example is the *Wire basket*, one of the pillars of our company's expansion into steel, this time reinvented in plastic (1997).

► Opposite, the historic objects Mari designed for Danese, since 1997 part of the Alessi catalogue: centre, the 1961 rectangular *Arran* tray, one of the symbols of Italian design.

▼ This *Learning game*, made in expanded polystyrene, has sixteen animals to fit together (1957).

Twergi and Tendentse

Twergi

● The other deep-rooted manufacturing tradition in the Strona valley, apart from metals, is small wooden items for home and kitchen. In our desire to return to these manufacturing roots, in 1988 we took over the valley's oldest original firm, Battista Piazza 1865. We have reproduced a number of historical items from the first few decades of this century, and revitalized the working of wood: our own designers and many young people have come up with a host of projects using many kinds of wood.

▲ The output of the Piazza firm was an industrial evolution of local crafts. The little elf, known as "twergi" in the Walser dialect, is the historic symbol of this. The good-natured little woodland sprite has been redesigned by Milton Glaser, who has set him on a tiny pair of skis.

▲ Dalisi's pointed *Grinder*
(1990–97)) keeps an eye
on Michael Graves's pearwood
Tray; Graves also made
the slim *Pepper mill* (1993).

◀ These pages contain
the "historical" utensils made
by Ubaldo Piazza in
the thirties, interspersed with
contemporary objects.

▶ The *Mirror* by Ico Migliore
and Mara Servetto (1992–98)
shyly withdraws before Milton
Glaser's *Lamp* (1989–97):
looking on are *Photo holders*
by Kuno Prey (1990).

▼ Ettore Sottsass fell in love
with the *Twergi* wood: all
the table articles below are
his (1989).

ALESSI

▲ The twin *Portrait holders* (1992–98), inspired by cartoons, bear Guido Venturini's unmistakable touch. The placid cherry wood *Newspaper holder* (1992–98) is by Ico Migliore and Mara Servetto. The steel and wooden *Trolley* (opposite) is by Adalberto Pironi (1996), and doubles as a TV stand. Below, the range of articles designed with a pinch of irreverence by Andrea Branzi, with lozenge decorations (1991–94). These designs are some of the projects developed by Sottsass, attentive as ever to all aspects of life at the table, right down to the tiniest pieces such as *Egg cups*, *Bottle tops* and *Napkin rings*.

● Tendentse was set up in Livorno to manufacture small articles, principally experimenting with new departures in majolica and porcelain. The first collection included works by Branzi, Cibic, De Lucchi, Gili, Mendini, Morozzi, Mutoh, Nannetti, Nardi, Natalini, Puppa, Raggi, Shama and Tarshito and Sottsass, today all out of production. Since 1989 Tendentse has been part of Alessi.

Tendentse

100% Make Up

● The metaproject of this venture, overseen by Alessandro Mendini, is the production of an ideal aesthetic factory, understood as a multiplication of individuals, as a sequence of aesthetic creatures all resembling one another. To obtain difference from the identical, one hundred authors worked on a single starting shape: in 1992 each finished article was produced in a run of 100, numbered from 1 to 10,000 and signed by all the designers at the same time.

" The decorations are like fishes in the sea: they exist even if you can't see them. "

▲ Mendini designed the standard gold-coloured vase (number 58 in the series), as well as various other possible decorations and stagings of the hundred vases, drawing ironic inspiration from various sequences or display possibilities.

▲ 1) Antonio Abate 2) Carla Accardi 3) Sanchita Ajjampur 4) Yael Applefeld
5) Quinuajuaq Ashewak 6) Paolo Bertozzi and Stefano Del Monte Casoni
7) Gabriel Bien-Aimé 8) Lapo Binazzi 9) Alighiero Boetti 10) Andreas Brandolini
11) Frédéric Bruly Bouabré 12) Sergio Calatroni 13) Juli Capella
14) Sergio Cappelli and Patrizia Ranzo 15) Nigel Coates 16) Cocktail
17) Gianni Colombo 18) Riccardo Dalisi 19) Nicola De Maria 20) Jan Digerud.

▲ 21) Emmanuel Ekefrey 22) Brian Eno 23) Ellinor Flor 24) Dan Friedman 25) Elizabeth Fritsch
26) Piero Gaeta 27) Giorgio Galli and Beatrice Santiccioli 28) Louise Gibb 29) Piero Gilardi
30) Anna Gili 31) Milton Glaser 32) Michael Graves 33) Maria Christina Hamel
34) Jan Mohamed Hanif 35) Pitt Heinke 36) Yoshiki Hishinuma 37) Susan Holm
38) Yong Ping Huang 39) Aussi Jaffari 40) Christer Jonson.

◀ 41) Bodys Isek Kingelez
42) Inka Kivalo
43) Mark Kostabi
44) Randi Kristensen
45) Milan Kunc
46) Kunstflug
47) Shiro Kuramata
48) Quim Larrea
49) Cheikh Ledy
50) Stefan Lindfors.

ALESSI

▲ 51) Kamba Luesa 52) Esther Mahlangu 53) Valente Malangatana
54) Karel Malich 55) Massimo Mariani 56) Giusi Mastro 57) Kivuthi Mbuno
58) Alessandro Mendini 59) Antonio Miralda 60) Sergei Vladimir Mironenko
61) Alexandre Mocika 62) Paola Navone 63) Sinua Okayama 64) Luigi Ontani
65) Eikki Orvola 66) Salcido Javier Perez-Gil 67) Eduardo Pla 68) Plumcake
69) Giorgio Rava 70) Ravage.

▲ 71) Ronaldo Pereira Rego 72) Roberto Remi 73) Cheri Samba 74) Andreas Schulze
75) Suresh Sethi 76) Raja Babu Sharma 77) Jari Silvennoinen 78) Ettore Sottsass, Jr.
79) Gregorio Spini 80) Philippe Starck 81) Peter Struycken 82) Sybilla 83) Guillermo Tejeda
84) Cyprien Tokoudagba 85) Dagmar Trinks 86) Maurizio Turchet 87) Twins Seven Seven
88) Masanori Umeda 89) Hilde Vemren 90) Robert Venturi.

▶ 91) Guido Venturini
92) Nanda Vigo
93) Mara Voce
94) Acharya Vyakul
95) Brigitta Watz
96) Gisbert Weiss
97) Hannes Wettstein
98) Y.A. Y.A. Young Aspirations Young Artists
99) Leonid Yentus
100) Rhonda Zwillinger.

King-Kong Family

ALESSI

LE NARRACIÓ DEL DOIEN ITALIANO

ALESSI: UNE DYNASTIE D'OBJETS
TYPES, PROTOTYPES, PETITES SÉRIES, FIASCOS,
SUCCÈS, DE 1921 À 1994.

Hôtel de Galliffet
50, rue de Varenne - Paris

" We've had enough of erudite designers like Mendini or Branzi, you need to have a degree in architecture to understand their designs… we'd like to design things that appeal to Leo Castelli and to ordinary folk too. "

● In the late eighties, in his usual discreet manner Alessandro Mendini—an invaluable conduit of new talent— told me of two young architects from Florence. Stefano Giovannoni and Guido Venturini came to see me, very nervous, with a few sketches. They were two rather odd looking guys, and I felt that their playful and elementary poetics, often closely inspired by the formal style of cartoons, was full of potential. I had them shown around the factory and did my best to fill them in about us, our hopes and possibilities. They listened to me very attentively, and the next time they came back with a whole book crammed with design notes.

► Among their drawings I found a very straightforward tray, its edge perforated with a little man motif, like the ones children cut out with scissors. The *Girotondo* project (1989) went ahead without any particular hitches or special enthusiasm: nobody could have imagined this would become our best-selling tray!

ALESSI

King-Kong's "little men" appeared on the edges of articles that for us are "normal", part of the most consolidated Alessi tradition, such as our perforated *Trays* or *Baskets*. And then the little guys multiplied, invading new, unknown territories such as deskpads, colonizing objects like *Pencil cases* or *Bookmarks*, until their apotheosis in the *Jewelry-go-round* (1998).

To be honest, I think that the King-Kongs, despite their indubitable intuition and great flair, have been lucky too. They were spot on with the "playful style", they understood how important it is to work with "emotional codes", but above all the project came at the right time, and its place in the Alessi catalogue hit the spot.

With hindsight, I'd say it was a typical case of applying the "child code" to a catalogue like ours, until then dominated by the authority, status and *style* of great designer's masterpieces: a counterweight to the then emerging talents of Rossi, Graves and Starck.

▶ Alongside the expanding family of "little men", since 1994 we have also seen a range of *Baskets*, *Fruit bowls*, *Trays* and *Breadstick holders* of varying sizes, all perforated with a triangle and rhomboid motif.

ALESSI

CSA and Young Designers

LAURA

● The Alessi Research Centre (CSA) was set up in 1990 for two purposes: to draw up theoretical papers on topics associated with objects (to be published as books), and to coordinate work with young designers. Up until that time Alessi had only worked with "major designers", and I felt a certain degree of responsibility towards young, upcoming designers. Laura Polinoro, whom Mendini suggested, has done sterling work.

❝ It is not easy to describe this 'workshop': fertile, subtle, a place where, like in a fairytale everything seems possible, where you cannot see a beginning nor know how it will all end... ❞

▶ The pictures on this page are taken from a workshop held at the Helsinki University of Industrial and Applied Art in 1996 and in Tokyo in 1997.

CENTRO STUDI
ALESSI

Laura has brought
to Alessi the intuition
and semiological training
garnered at the school
of Eco and Fabbri.
She sometimes reminds
me of Marianne Brandt,
the first woman to work
at the Bauhaus
Metallwerkstatt during
the twenties.
Laura started the arduous
process of shaking Alessi
out of its contentedness
with a certain type of
high-flown Italian design.
Through her we have
brought new disciplines to
bear at Alessi, anthropology
and semiology to name but
two. Nine years on,
in 1998 the CSA of Milan
moved to Crusinallo.

◀ The CSA's design
management work takes
place principally through
workshops and design
seminars with students, in
collaboration with architecture
faculties and schools of art
and design, as well as with
groups of specially invited
designers. We have held
workshops all over the world:
in Argentina, England, Japan,
Brazil, Costa Rica, the U.S.,
Australia, France, Germany,
Finland, Austria, even in the
Aegean Islands.

In 1990 I too was seconded to this task, one which I undertake with great enthusiasm: these photographs show the workshop held at Miami University in 1996. Each year I do my best to set aside at least two periods to hold personal workshops. I have taken great pleasure in trying to teach young people about my field, and I'm curious to find out what they think about us, how they consider what Alessi is doing. The workshops are not just about teaching, they also play a significant operational role, sometimes leading to veritable projects, or else verifying the suitability of designs for manufacture. To sum up, it's a very interesting part of Alessi's open policy towards the concept of "metaproject", the creation of a structure of ongoing mental research.

▲ These two photos are of projects by Stella Böß (the *Entia* and *Challenger* perfume burners) and Christian Jurke (the *Crisute II* electric kettle), developed during the workshop held with Andreas Brandolini at the Hochschule der Bildenden Künste of Saarbrücken (1994–95).

Memory Containers Creole Project

● The first metaproject coordinated by CSA, opening up Alessi to young designers; to be precise, young women designers, as during the introductory phase around 200 women designers under 30 were invited from all over the world. The questions we were asking: what is expected of the object? How are objects born, how do they change when moving from one culture to another? What changes in their shape, perception, use?

How does an object become a cultural object? This was an exploration into the archetypes of presentation and "offering" of food and its rituals, with inspiration coming from the memory of a culture or a personal experience. The goal was to realize a "Creole" project, a test-tube cloning of that which,

given its natural span, happens much more slowly when different cultures come together.

▲ *Treats* goodies box by Anna Gili (1998), the *Helmut* citrus-basket by Cecilia Cassina, the *Chimu* table centre-piece bowl by Joanna Lyle and Susan Cohn's pierced *Basket* (1992–94).

◀ In the heat of the moment, *Inneres Feuer*, the chafing-dish with candle designed by Vera Purtscher (1997).

▼ *Tundra* is the poetic trivet with reindeer, designed by Kristiina Lassus (1995).

▶ Here, Clare Brass's three *Kalistò* kitchen boxes. Below, *Brasero*, a chafing-dish with candles, designed by Maria Sanchez, next to *Tin man*, a kitchen box with a wooden knob, by Constantin Boym (1992–94).

ALESSI

Memory Containers | **Biological Project**

◀ The relationship between steel and glass looms large in Biological Project. To the side, Pierangelo Caramia's *Bisquit box* and Theo Williams's *Honey pot* (1995). Below, Joanna Lyle's *Kitchen boxes* bottom, beneath Alejandro Ruiz's *Parmenides* parmesan cheese grater (1994), is the *Oggetto dell'equilibrio*, a set for perfuming and restoring balance to the home (1996).

● This chapter examines a new vein of research: the discovery of Es, in a primary concept, of perception, more closely associated with intuition and receptive capabilities than the expression of different cultures through stylistic languages.
The goal is to unearth new relationships linking the rule and the project: the living, vital object wins the man and nature conflict.

● The metaproject F.F.F., begun in 1991, grew out of a desire to explore the emotional structure of objects even more profoundly than we had done in the past. We were interested in the most delicate, intimate, sensory human needs. The objects became ludic tools, telling little tales, giving captivating twists to everyday uses, suggesting a mediation with playfulness... they become a bridge to the fantastical.

F.F.F. Family Follows Fiction

▲ The *Mix Italia* espresso coffee maker (1993) was one of the last joint projects by the King-Kong duo.

▶ Thanks to its allusive shape and the instinctive sense of empathy and familiarity it breeds, *Penguin Tea* with its special *Happy Egg* (1993), is one of F.F.F.'s symbol-objects. The objects by Venturini and Giovannoni in the picture above are also part of this research.

ALESSI

◀ The *Coniglio Mattia* (1998) is an electronic timer/clock in different coloured resins, designed by Mattia Di Rosa.

◀ A colour resin version of Christopher Dresser's historic *Sugar bowl* (1864).

For F.F.F. we drew upon Winnicott's words on "transitional objects", as well as Franco Fornari's "theory of emotional codes". At the outset the idea was to reproduce the process of creation and animation of the object common to the world of childhood, and to primitive cultures.

▶ The stars of these pages are the amusing little devil *Bottle-openers* by Biagio Cisotti (1994), Mattia Di Rosa's laughing little creatures (*Timer/clock, Pressure caps, Napkin rings, Kitchen boxes,* the raised cake stand *Bimboveloce*), Enrica Zanzi's *Photo holder heart* (1996) and *So & Zò*, Stefano Pirovano's playful half-moon (1998).

FRONTE

PROFILO

▼ Another F.F.F. product/character, in production starting in 1998, is the *Folpo* (which in Veneto dialect means octopus, as can be seen from the tentacles of the little tame creatures) glass whisk cum measurer by Marta Sansoni.

b.b. baby bathroom

●Could it be true? Dentists have been quoted as saying that if the young generation has caries, they will all feel like failures. Well... this hasn't stopped us from attempting to make dental hygiene more fun for children (and adults too) with a family of colourful characters made out of thermo-plastic rubber designed by Stefano Pirovano (1998). The new design project

b.b. baby bathroom includes *Rondo*, a lid for toothpaste tubes, *Otto*, an interdental thread, and *Sden*, a matching set of two toothbrush covers. As for fighting on the front line of caries prevention, we'll leave that to manufacturers of candy, chocolates, toffee, chewing gum and so on; not to mention manufacturers of drills!

Stefano Giovannoni

" But who is this Michael Graves? He's certainly not a designer! "

● A "born again" designer par excellence, bearing a vague resemblance to a rumpled teddy bear, a man who looks like he might be anything except a much-acclaimed designer, Stefano conceals one of the most explosive talents I have ever had the good fortune to come across. He is not happy that we classify him as "one of the young", he feels he is destined for the designer hall of fame, and he wants to have his share of acclaim with my "masters". He'll no doubt get there, even if a little grizzly and impatient at times.

◀ The *Mary biscuit* boxes and the *Molly* kitchen scales (1995) speak a soft, flowing language: with such sweet and soft dispositions, I am convinced that all Giovannoni's objects look at us affectionately with the mysterious yet warm smile of the *Mona Lisa*, "that smile associated with the sentiment of beauty which in adulthood moves the human heart, which for all of us, when falling in love or glimpsing a beautiful thing, is apparently associated with the intense visual relationship established with our mother's face, constituted as representative of the intra-uterine bliss" (Frontori, 1986).

ALESSI

▲The trivets in the *Coins* range (1995) are like outsize coins bearing explicit legends.

▼ The meticulous research conducted by Marco Migliari and Marco Millozza into the types and natures of herbs and spices (powdered, leaf, in pieces, in grains) has led to the birth of a table-top botanical garden: the lids of Giovannoni's *Spice pots* (1997) remind us of what is inside: nutmeg, cloves, chili pepper, parsley, oregano, bay leaves, basil…

▲ The *Nutty the cracker* nutcracker (1993) is an example of how Giovannoni works, his finger on the pulse of our emotional codes, in particular that of the mother and child.

▶ *Lilliput* (1993) is Giovannoni's highly original and inventive salt and pepper set. The two containers have magnetic feet which stick to the base.

▲ *Fruit Mama*: a big, welcoming hand holding up the fruit, or is it a "new apple tree"? Definitely another non-anonymous presence in the house, which Giovannoni wishes to animate with a thousand characters of all hues (1993).

▼ The cartoon effect reaches its apogee with the infamous *Merdolino* (1993). Without pulling his punches, Giovannoni tackles an indispensable but "taboo" object, the toilet brush, turning it into a slender vase from which sprouts a long, allusive and inviting shrub.

ALESSI

▶ *Ship Shape* (1998) is a creative container: it can be used for sauces, butter, jams… Sweet or savoury, it comes with a ready-to-use spatula for your imaginative delights.

▼ An international character with a long-standing pedigree in texts on pedagogy and psychoanalysis, Pinocchio is now a long-nosed funnel, the smiling *Pino* (1998): truth or lie?

▶ Among so many festive eating rites, there is one lonely and melancholic pastime: breaking into a boiled egg, an act which is usually performed in reluctant intimacy, in a deep silence broken only by those tentative blows to the shell, making the humble boiled egg almost a metaphor for crepuscular solitude. Giovannoni has managed to brighten this moment up, make it a playful and gregarious thing with *Coccodandy* (1998), his basket for cooking eggs, which comes with four highly coloured recesses for cooking and serving eggs to friends.

◄ Ex-children may recall a small and well-loved cartoon character called Grisù, a little dragon always busy trying to remedy the damage caused by the fire he inadvertently breathes. We trust that those who get to grips with the long neck of this diminutive household dragon *Bruce*, will be more careful with this hot item, a table lighter (1998).

► Toothpicks may be indispensable, but they can be embarrassing to use: to put a light touch to what is not a particularly refined gesture, Giovannoni pulls out a rabbit from the unpredictable top hat of his creativity: the *Magic Bunny* toothpick holder (1998).

◄ *Macaroni, you've pushed me to the limit and now I'm going to eat you!* This is how Italian comic Alberto Sordi enjoined battle with a huge plate of steaming pasta. *Rigatone* is an invitation to eat Mediterranean-style, a kitchen box for spaghetti designed by Giovannoni (1998), whose shape and "topping" (a tomato lid) mimic what is probably Italy's best-known dish.

ALESSI

▶ The *Alibaba* (1998) jug with vacuum glass poses an intriguing question: why this particular name? Let's hazard a guess. In the cave of the forty thieves, the hero of this Oriental fairytale hides inside a rounded earthenware jar, from which the top of his turban pokes out: Stefano Giovannoni—a philologist of the fairy tale—is perhaps summoning up this image.

◀ Mnemonic references are far clearer for the *Rimini* cutlery drainer (1998). The visual pointer is explicit and heart-warming: that old bucket abandoned so many times on a beach with its spade and sand moulds.

▼ The *Big Clip* photo-frame (1998) recalls one of the most typical expedients of estrangement: an everyday object which "emerges" from its everyday level, taking on an unusual dimension and changing function. And so a simple paper spring holder becomes an original frame.

▼ *Mami* (1999) is the third set
of saucepans in the history of Alessi,
after *La Cintura di Orione* by Sapper
and *Falstaf* by Mendini. This time
I entrusted to a young designer the
difficult task of stimulating people's
imagination by exploring the archaic
world of "kitchenware". The spelt soup
bubbles once again in the earthenware
jar, and the capacious, rotund and
sacred pots "with two ears"
(as Catullus wrote) evoke the warmth
of bygone eras. The truly complete set,
in complete harmony with Giovannoni's
"poetics of the emotions", includes also
the *Frying pans* and *Beafsteak pans*
in non-stick cast aluminium.

ALESSI

Guido Venturini

" Fields of expression such as art, music and cinema allow you to get out the nasty, ugly, violent things, because of their nature providing a release. Design does not usually offer such opportunities… "

● Guido is a committed explorer of the "Twilight Zone". His objects are highly expressive characters: wild, certainly out of the ordinary, vaguely monstrous but never threatening, indeed, to me they look like they're asking our assistance. Guido does a lot of thinking about the role of the designer in today's society, he is aware of the contradictions inherent in our work: I like seeing his work as that of a conscientious objector. Good old Guido, we'll travel far together, as long as you don't get lost along the way!

▲ In stainless steel or in blue and yellow, the *Wardance* tray (1998) is decorated in a rather disconcerting manner: a perfect recipient for poisoned apples, it might help to bring back the historical position of taster.

◀ The very well-built *Antonio* (1997) shows off his powerful muscles in a body-building clothes-rack.

◀ The *Nonno di Antonio* garlic-squeezer and *Fred Worm* jug with vacuum glass (1997). Guido's designs are so anthropomorphic that the other day we received an e-mail from Dallas, Texas, from a certain Fred Worm asking us to pay him a royalty for using his name...

◀ *Gino Zucchino* (1993) a sugar sifter, but at Alessi it has become so popular it has turned into a kind of garden gnome.

ALESSI

Alessi gioca col fuoco.

◀ This gas-lighter is called *Firebird* (1993), but the name is not a homage to Stravinsky. It is one of the most explicit and "courageous" of all the characters in the Alessi catalogue, an ironic reference to the "erotic code".

Historical Reproductions

● When reviewing the history of the applied arts, especially that of smaller household articles, I never cease to be amazed by the substantial invariability of standard models: a goblet, a tray or a spoon are the fruit of an ongoing virtual work in progress conducted by a few hundred designers over thousands of years of human history. Almost all the objects we work with have ancient origins, and are strongly conditioned by rituals, plucked either from memory or the collective unconscious. We present some of these past designs in this chapter, illustrating creative moments, historical epochs and prototypes by major creators in our own specific field.

◄ With the aid of Neapolitan architects and archaeologists, in 1997 we reconstructed a scale model steel tray for this small first-century A.D. Roman bronze sculpture of a jester/focaccia hawker, found at the *House of Ephebus* at Pompeii, conserved at the Naples Archaeological Museum.

Christopher Dresser

▲ Dresser's many objects (the *Teapots*, the *Cruet sets*, the *Parmesan cheese-butter bowl with ice holder*) show he was always far ahead of his time.

● Dresser (1834–1904) was a well-regarded English botanist and scholar of the decorative arts who was probably the first industrial designer in the modern sense of the term. Unlike his Arts & Crafts Movement contemporaries, he wholeheartedly accepted all the implications of industrial mass-production, harnessing this to the design of bold, highly visionary crafted objects.

▶ This *Toast-rack* (1878), manufactured in stainless steel in 1991, has functional lines that are a foretaste of the Bauhaus spirit.

▲ Dresser was a prime example of the Moderate Transgression I seek in design. His projects show he knew the techniques of metal production better than any designer who has come to Alessi, and it is no coincidence that some of the objects we have chosen to "reproduce" are naturals for manufacture in modern day stainless steel.

This did not prevent him from never accepting the technical as a goal; he constantly probed boundaries as he sought higher expressive and constructive results. Some of these results, such as his *Triangular teapot* (designed in 1880 and produced in 1991) with legs, are even unsettling, while others show daring levels of intellectual and professional openness.

Staatliches Bauhaus

● Founded by Walter Gropius in Weimar in 1919 as a school of art and applied arts, subsequently directed by Hannes Meyer and Mies van der Rohe, Bauhaus is one of the historic workshops whose *mission* Alessi hopes to share. The reproductions on these pages are by Hans Przyrembel, Marianne Brandt, Otto Rittweger and Josef Knau. Because of the great talents of the people

involved, because of its stated desire to develop a practice founded on the principle "Art and Engineering: a new unity" at the very moment the problem of reproducing works of art was a passionate topic of debate, because of the obstacles thrown up by conservative opponents and later by Nazism, Bauhaus was one of the legendary originators of the Modern Movement in architecture and design.

▶ The designs shown on these pages were created at the Bauhaus Metallwerkstatt between 1924 and 1930, prevantly under the tutelage of Lazló Moholy-Nagy (seen here with Marianne Brandt). They are manufactured under license from the Bauhaus Archiv in Berlin. On the facing page, the sleek *Tea doser* (Hans Przyrembel, 1926), *Sugar and creamer set* (Marianne Brandt and Helmut Schulze, 1926), and the *Set of two tea infusers* (Otto Rittweger and Josef Knau, 1924), all made in 1995. In the middle, the *Tea and coffee service* (Marianne Brandt, 1924), manufactured in 1985.

▼In a photo self-portrait which has become famous, Marianne Brandt, who made all the works on this page, "wears" metal items as if they were jewels.

▶ A leading figure in the shift to the modern in Finnish objects and architecture, Eliel Saarinen (1873–1950) had an organic and unitary vision of design: using simple geometric shapes (adapted, incidentally, from industrial processing) Saarinen broke a great deal of new ground with the concept of "domestic landscape". This silver *Tea set with urn*, we produced in 1987, is considered one of the archetypes of American design.

Eliel Saarinen

Piero Bottoni

◀ The *Modular element candies bowl* (1991), designed around 1928 is an exemplary Piero Bottoni piece: elegant rationalism, in no way self-satisfied, displaying clear classic lines yet totally practical. It is very moving to see an object made up of a cone and circle mutate into a living shape through the arrangement of its components.

▶ Designed in 1938 and unveiled (in silver) at the 1940 Triennale, the *Caccia* cutlery range was considered a splendid example of "Lombard classicism" in the world and was praised by Gio Ponti due to the masterful balance struck between the craft past and the industrial future of household objects.

Luigi Caccia Dominioni, Livio & Pier Giacomo Castiglioni

◀ Thanks to an agreement with the Castiglioni heirs, this cutlery is now reproduced in silver plated nickel-silver and in steel (1990): Luigi Caccia Dominioni himself oversaw completion of the series, designing the items missing from the original project fifty years later.

ALESSI

Pio Manzù

▲ Designed in 1966 as a gadget for Fiat, *Cronotime* is a highly effective example of sixties design, pared down and typically "industrial" in its materials and colours. The two cylindrical sections can be turned to alter its shape. The deliberate declaration of function and use reflects Pio Manzù's training at the "legendary" Ulm School of Design.

▼ Designed in 1970, the *Optic* alarm-clock is a small but highly important product of Joe Colombo's creativity. As an object it is self-standing and laden with suggestive echoes; it is also a piece of the broader mosaic of a speculative future "integrated home" project.

Joe Colombo

ALESSI

The Alessi Museum

▲ Setting up an Alessi Museum is a physiological evolution in a two-decade-long process of theme and solution development. Many of the publications that have come out over this period presaged this outcome, if nothing else for the intrinsic, captivating poetic and artistic riches of this wealth of projects, for the density of intellectual debate from which they have emerged. Nevertheless, the Museum has opened its doors at a unique time, in a climate where the very function of museums is at a crossroads. The Museum is part of a phenomenon that is spontaneous and curious: Alessi is taking on the age/nature/identity of a museum, a novel kind of museum.

● Our role as a "Factory of Italian Design", somewhere between manufacturing and art, has gradually attracted the attention of museums of applied arts and industrial design from all over the world, and there have been many exhibitions of our work. Thanks to our constant experimentation over the years, we have produced a vast and fascinating body of prototypes which, together with our historical output and countless objects collected over the decades from all over the globe, form a valuable cross-section of the history of our field and our aims.

The Alessi Museum, opened in spring 1998, has been built to house all the objects, designs, images and documents of all types regarding the history of Alessi and, more generally, the history of household articles. This new museum has come into being within our own structure; it is destined to reinforce our metaproject outlook and production policy (through the support of historical authorities), as well as provide a more direct and comprehensive channel for communicating with the museums we have been working with for some time. Designed by Mendini and curated by Francesca Appiani, the Alessi Museum is open to researchers, scholars, journalists and students.

ALESSI

◀ Alessi's cultural output also includes a now extensive series of scientific and research publications, listed in the bibliography here. Some of these works have become "classics", opening up international debates on the future prospects and forms of expression of design.

ALESSI

▶ Alessandro Mendini has designed installations for various Alessi exhibitions: this page, below, the polymorphous organism for new products at the Milan showroom. Hans Hollein designed the display for the *Tea & Coffee Piazza* project (right) with the now famous split arch, as well as the major "Paesaggio casalingo" exhibition, presenting Alessi's output from 1921 to 1980, opening at the Milan Triennale in December 1979, travelling to Linz and Berlin in 1980.

▲ Pictures of Alessi exhibitions in Paris, Sydney and Tel Aviv recall the many shows held in museums all over the world: "Paesaggio casalingo" (Milan, Linz, Berlin 1979–81); "Tea & Coffee Piazza" (United States, Milan, Krefeld, Zurich, Aachen, Barcelona, Kyoto, Ghent, Antwerp (1983–86); "La Conica e altre caffettiere" (Milan 1983); "Tafelarchitektur" (Rotterdam, Düsseldorf 1985); "Création" (Lyon 1986); "La caffettiera e Pulcinella" (Milan 1987); "Not in production / Next to production" (Milan, Ghent 1988–90); "L'atelier Alessi" (Paris, Brussels, Scandinavia, Brazil, Zagreb 1989–95); "100% Make Up"

(Florence, Ghent, Groningen, Roanne, Nice (1992–93); "Alessi 1921–1994" (France 1994); Manger (Vevey 1994); "For the sake of use" (Tel Aviv 1994); "F.F.F." (Ljubljana 1995); "Achille Castiglioni Designer" (Barcelona-Milan-Bergamo-Weil am Rhein-New York-Tokyo-Niitsu-Breda 1995–98); "Starckologie" (Frankfurt, Paris 1996); "Metallarbeiten" (Berlin 1996); "Omaggio ad Aldo Rossi" (Milan-Hamburg 1998); "Alessi" (New York 1998); "Alessi, The Dream Factory" (Caracas 1998).

▲ Set up in a building inside the Crusinallo factory complex, the museum displays a huge number of prototypes, products no longer in production, graphics, blueprints and prints covering the history of Alessi. Also, machinery, engravings, designer installations, historic photos, books, magazines and catalogues. It is a veritable specialist museum of twentieth century applied art and design, with a number of very rare exhibits; what's more, it also serves as an ordered archive of Alessi's cultural identity.

Bibliography

XI Triennale, exhibition catalogue (Milan, Triennale), Milan 1957.

Carmelo Cappello, exhibition catalogue, Messina 1973.

XV Triennale, exhibition catalogue (Milan, Triennale), Milan 1973.

Dušan Džamonja. Sculture, disegni e progetti dal 1963 al 1974, exhibition catalogue, Milan 1975.

A. Pansera, *Storia e cronaca della Triennale*, Longanesi, Milan 1978.

Design & Design, exhibition catalogue of the XIth Compasso d'oro, ADI, Milan 1979.

A. Mendini, *Paesaggio casalingo. La produzione Alessi nell'industria dei casalinghi dal 1921 al 1980*, Domus, Milan 1979.

E. Sottsass, *Esercizio formale*, exhibition catalogue, Alessi, Crusinallo 1979.

XVI Triennale, exhibition catalogue (Milan, Triennale 1979–1982), Alinari, Florence.

Centrokappa, Il design italiano negli anni '50, Domus, Milan 1980.

Diseñadores Industriales Italianos 1980, exhibition catalogue (Buenos Aires, Universidad de Buenos Aires, Facultad de Arquitectura y urbanismo), Buenos Aires 1980.

A. Grassi and A. Pansera, *Atlante del design italiano 1940–1980*, Fabbri, Milan 1980.

Var. Authors, *Design ist unsichtbar*, exhibition catalogue, Löcker Verlag, Vienna 1980.

B. Radice, *Elogio del banale*, Alchimia, Milan 1980.

Bio 9, Bienale Industrijskega Oblikovanja, exhibition catalogue, Bio, Ljubljana 1981.

A. Mendini, *Architettura addio*, Shakespeare & Company, Milan 1981.

XII Compasso d'oro, exhibition catalogue, Electa, Milan 1981.

P. Arnell, T. Bickford and K. Vogel Wheeler, *Michael Graves. Buildings and Projects 1966–1981*, Rizzoli International, New York 1982.

F. Burkhardt, *Cibi e riti–Essen und Ritual*, Proceedings of the design seminar held at the IDZ in Berlin, Alessi, Crusinallo 1982.

V. Gregotti, *Il disegno nel prodotto industriale. Italia 1960–1980*, Electa, Milan, 1982.

F. Irace, *Precursors of Post Modernism–Milan 1920–30's*, exhibition catalogue, The Architectural League, New York 1982.

Italian Re-Evolution, exhibition catalogue (La Jolla Museum of Contemporary Art), Milan 1982.

Provokationen–Design aus Italien. Ein Mythos geht neue Wege, exhibition catalogue (Hannover, Deutscher Werkbund), Hannover 1982.

Var. Authors, *Conseguenze impreviste–Arte, moda, design*, exhibition catalogue (Florence), Electa, Milan 1982, vol. III.

Var. Authors, *Gli anni trenta. Arte e cultura italiana*, exhibition catalogue, Mazzotta, Milan 1982.

Var. Authors, *Nuove intenzioni del design*, R.D.E., Milan 1982.

Dal cucchiaio alla città nell'itinerario di 100 designer, exhibition catalogue, Electa, Milan 1983.

Design, exhibition catalogue (Zurich, Kunstgewerbemuseum), Zurich 1983.

Design Experimenta Preview '83, exhibition catalogue, Todi 1983.

Design since 1945, exhibition catalogue (Philadelphia, Museum of Art), Rizzoli International, New York 1983.

Icsid design Milan, exhibition catalogue, R.D.E., vol. IV, Milan 1983.

C. Mann, *Clotet–Tusquets*, Gustavo Gili, Barcelona 1983.

A. Mendini, *Progetto infelice*, R.D.E., Milan 1983.

Var. Authors, *Officina Alessi. Tea & Coffee Piazza*, Shakespeare & Company, Milan 1983.

Bio 10, Bienale Industrijskega Oblikovanja, exhibition catalogue, Bio, Ljubljana 1984.

Castiglioni A. Meister des Design der Gegenwart, exhibition catalogue, Electa, Milan 1984.

Memphis Design, Kruithuis, s'Hertogebosch 1984.

A. Rossi, *La conica e altre caffettiere*, Alessi, Crusinallo 1984.

Tre anni di design, XIII Compasso d'oro, exhibition catalogue, R.D.E., Milan 1984.

Var. Authors, *L'economia italiana tra le due guerre 1919–1939*, exhibition catalogue, Ipsoa, Roma 1984.

P. Arnell and T. Bickford, *Aldo Rossi. Buildings and Projects*, Rizzoli International, New York 1985.

A. Bangert, *Italienisches Möbeldesign. Klassiker von 1945 bis 1985*, Modernes Design, München 1985.

S. Bayley, *The Conran Dictionary of Design*, Conran Octopus, London 1985.

P.C. Bontempi and G. Gregori, *Alchimia*, Copi, The Hague 1985.

Dalla tartaruga all'arcobaleno, exhibition catalogue, (Milan, Triennale), Triennale-Electa, Milan 1985.

Ettore Sottsass, Mobili e qualche arredamento. Furniture and a few Interiors, exhibition catalogue, Mondadori-Daverio, Milan 1985.

H. Hollein, *Hans Hollein*, exhibition catalogue, A+U Publishing, Tokyo 1985.

R. Horn, *Memphis–Objects, Furniture and Patterns*, Running Press, Philadephia 1985.

S. Kohmoto, *Contemporary Landscape. From The Horizon of Post Modern Design*, exhibition catalogue (Kyoto, The National Museum of Modern Art).

Louisiana Revy, no. 3, 1985.

E. Medagliani and F. Gosetti, *Pastario ovvero atlante delle paste alimentari italiane*, Alessi, Crusinallo 1985.

K. Sato, *Alchimia, Never Ending Italian Design*, Rikuyo-sha, Tokyo 1985.

P. Scarzella, *Il bel metallo. Storia dei casalinghi nobili della Alessi*, Arcadia, Milan 1985.

R. Stern, *The International Design Yearbook 1985–1986*, Thames and Hudson, London 1985.

Strategie d'intesa, exhibition catalogue, Electa, Milan 1985.

H. Wichmann, *Die neue Sammlung. Ein neuer Museumstyp des 20. Jahrhunderts*, exhibition catalogue, Prestel, Munich 1985.

E. Ambasz, *The International Design Yearbook 1986–1987*, Thames and Hudson, London 1986.

A table, exhibition catalogue (Paris, Centre Georges Pompidou), Paris 1986.

Bio 11, Bienale Industrijskega Oblikovanja, exhibition catalogue, Bio, Ljubljana 1986.

Caravelles. L'enjeu de l'objet, exhibition catalogue, Grenoble–Lyons–Saint-Etienne 1986.

A. Grassi and A. Pansera, *L'Italia del design. Trent'anni di dibattito*, Marietti, Casale Monferrato 1986.

Italia Diseño 1946–1986, exhibition catalogue (Museo Rufino Tamayo), Mexico 1986.

R. Krause, V. Pasca and I. Vercelloni, *La mossa del cavallo. Mobili e oggetti oltre il design*, Condé Nast, Milan 1986.

Semenzato Nuova Geri, asta di modernariato 1900–1986, Passigli, Milan 1986.

Teyssot, il progetto domestico. La casa dell'uomo: archetipi e prototipi, exhibition catalogue (Milan, XVIIth Triennale), Electa, Milan 1986.

Var. Authors, *Les carnets du design. Les arts de la table*, Mad-Cap, Paris 1986.

A. Alessi and A. Gozzi, *La cintura di Orione*, Longanesi, Milan 1987.

J. Capella and Q. Larrea, *Diseño de Arquitectos en los 80*, Gustavo Gili, Barcelona, 1987.

M. Collins, *Towards Post-Modernism: Design since 1985*, British Museum Publications, London 1987.

R. Dalisi, *La caffettiera e Pulcinella. Ricerca sulla caffettiera napoletana 1979–1987*, Officina Alessi, Crusinallo, 1987.

Hans Hollein. Metaphores et metamorphes, exhibition catalogue (Paris, Centre Georges Pompidou), Paris 1987.

H. Klotz, *Jahrbuch für Architektur 1987–1988*, Deutches Architekturmuseum, Frankfurt 1987.

S. von Moos, *Venturi Rauch & Scott Brown*, Rizzoli International, New York 1987.

B. Munari, M. Bellini and A. Branzi, *Descendants of Leonardo da Vinci. The Italian Design*, Graphic-Sha, Tokyo 1987.

Nouvelles tendences. Les avant-gardes de la fin du XXᵉ siècle, exhibition catalogue (Paris, Centre Georges Pompidou), Paris 1987.

XIV Premio Compasso d'oro, exhibition catalogue, Silvia, Milan 1987.

A. Rossi, *Aldo Rossi Architect*, Electa, Milan 1987.

D. Sudjic, *The International Design Yearbook 1987–1988*, Thames and Hudson, London 1987.

Var. Authors, *The Post Modern Object*, exhibition catalogue, Ga Pindar, London 1987.

A. Alessi, *Not In Production–Next To Production,* exhibition catalogue, Alessi, Crusinallo 1988.

Bio 12, Bienale Indusrijskega Oblikovanja, exhibition catalogue, Bio, Ljubljana 1988.

G. Bosoni and F.G. Confalonieri, *Paesaggio del design italiano 1972–1988*, Edizioni di Comunità, Milan 1988.

C. Colin, *Design d'aujourd'hui*, Flammarion, Paris 1988.

C. Colin, *Starck*, Pierre Mardaga Editeur, Liège 1988.

Der Verzeichnete Promotheus, exhibition catalogue, Nishen Verlag, Berlin 1988.

Design in Catalogna, exhibition catalogue, BCD, Barcelona 1988.

I. Favata, *Joe Colombo, Designer 1930–1971*, exhibition catalogue, Idea Books, Milan 1988.

F. Fischer, *Design Heute*, exhibition catalogue (Frankfurt, Deutsches Architekturmuseum), Frankfurt 1988.

C. Gambardella, *Il progetto leggero. Riccardo Dalisi: vent'anni di design*, Clean, Naples 1988.

F. Haks, *Alessandro Mendini Sketsboek–Sketches*, Froukje Hoekstra, Amsterdam 1988.

Arata Isozaki, *The International Design Yearbook 1988–1989*, Thames and Hudson, London 1988.

B. Klesse, *Hundert Jahre Museum für Angewandte Kunst der Gegenwart. Mäzenatentum*, exhibition catalogue, (Cologne, Museum für Angewandte Kunst), Cologne 1988.

La caffettiera napoletana e Pulcinella, exhibition catalogue (Taranto, Circolo Italsider), Editrice Scorpione, Taranto 1988.

R. Sambonet, *L'arte in tavola*, Industria Grafica Ronda, Milan 1988.

S. San Pietro and M. Vercelloni, *Nuovi negozi a Milan*, L'Archivolto, Milan 1988.

Richard Sapper. 40 Progetti di Design 1958–1988, exhibition catalogue, Arti Grafiche Mazzucchelli, Milan 1988.

Penny Sparke, *Italienisches Design*, Thames and Hudson, London 1988.

H. Wichmann, *Italian Design 1945 bis heute*, Die Neue Sammlung, Munich 1988.

Var. Authors, *Alessandro Mendini*, exhibition catalogue (Groningen, Groninger Museum), Giancarlo Politi, Milan 1988.

Var. Authors, *Design und Wohnen,* exhibition catalogue, Helga Treft, Frankfurt 1988.

Var. Authors, *Sottsass Associates*, Rizzoli International, New York, 1988.

M. Collins and A. Papadakis, *Post-Modern Design*, Rizzoli International, New York 1989.

P. and R. Colombari, *Effetto acciaio*, exhibition catalogue, Arti Grafiche Giacone, Turin 1989.

Compasso d'oro. Italian Design, exhibition catalogue, Silvia

Editore, Milan 1989.

XV Premio Compasso d'oro, exhibition catalogue, Silvia Editrice, Milan 1989.

G. Lueg, *Design*, exhibition catalogue (Cologne, Museum für Angewandte Kunst), Cologne 1989.

L. Peel, P. Powell and A. Garrett, *An Introduction to 20th Century Architecture*, Quinted Publishing, London 1989.

L. Polinoro, *L'Officina Alessi. Alberto Alessi e Alessandro Mendini: dieci anni di progetto, 1980-1990*, F.A.O., Crusinallo 1989.

Var. Authors, *Alessandro Mendini*, exhibition catalogue, Giancarlo Politi, Milan 1989.

Var. Authors, *From Matt Black to Memphis and back again*, Blueprint/Wordsearch, London 1989.

Var. Authors, *Role of Design, V. Design for a Coming Age*, JIDPO, Tokyo 1989.

Var. Authors, *Von Außen von Innen. 25 Modus Jahre*, Modus Möbel, Berlin 1989.

A. Bangert and K.M. Armer, *Design der 80er Jahre*, Bangert Verlag, Munich 1990.

N. Bellati, *New Italian Design*, Rizzoli International, New York 1990.

M. Bellini, *The International Design Yearbook 1990–1991*, Thames and Hudson, London 1990.

Collezione per un modello di museo del disegno industriale italiano, exhibition catalogue, Fabbri, Milan 1990.

European Community Design Prize 1990, exhibition catalogue, BCD, Barcelona 1990.

L. Gobbi, F. Morace, R. Brognara and F. Valente, *I Boom*, Lupetti & Co. Editore, Milan 1990.

W. Halen, *Christopher Dresser*, Christies, Oxford 1990.

Juli Capella & Quim Larrea, Oscar Tusquets objects dans le parc, exhibition catalogue, Gustavo Gili, Barcelona 1990.

Metall für den Gaumen, exhibition catalogue, beim Herausgeber, Vienna 1990.

J. Myerson and S. Katz, *Kitchenware*, Conran Octopus, London 1990.Var. Authors, *Michael Graves. Buildings and Projects, 1982–1989*, Princeton Architectural Press, Princeton 1990.

A. Rowland, *Bauhaus Source Book*, Quarto, London 1990.

Var. Authors, *Aldo Rossi Architecture 1981–1991*, Princeton Architectural Press, New York 1991.

Var. Authors, *Architetture elettriche*, Biticino, Milan 1991.

Var. Authors, *Christopher Dresser*, F.A.O., Crusinallo 1991.

Var. Authors, *New and Notable Product Design*, Rockport Publishers, Rockport 1991.

A. Branzi, *Il dolce Stil Novo (della casa)*, F.A.O., Crusinallo 1991.

J. Capella and Q. Larrea, *Nuevo diseño español*, Gustavo Gili, Barcelona 1991.

O. Boissiere, *Starck*, Taschen Verlag, Cologne 1991.

S. Casciani and G. Di Pietrantonio, *Design in Italia 1950–1990*, Giancarlo Politi, Milan 1991.

R. Dalisi, *L'oggetto eroticomiko*, F.A.O., Crusinallo 1991.

P. Dormer, *The Illustrated Dictionary of Twentieth Century Designers*, Quarto Publishing, London 1991.

Formes des metropoles–Nouveaux designs en Europe, exhibition catalogue (Paris, Centre Georges Pompidou), Paris 1991.

P. Polato, *Il modello nel design*, Hoepli, Milan 1991.

L. Polinoro, *Rebus sic...* , F.A.O., Crusinallo 1991.

Primavera del disseny. Barcelona 1991 Spring Design, exhibition catalogue (Barcelona, Ajuntament de Barcelona), Barcelona 1991.

2e Quadriennale Internationale de Design, exhibition catalogue, Caravelles 2, Lyons 1991.

A. Mendini, *La fabbrica estetica*, F.A.O., Crusinallo1992.

Casa Barcelona, exhibition catalogue, IMPI, Barcelona 1992.

A. Ferlenga, *Aldo Rossi Architetture 1988–1992*, Electa, Milan 1992.

Nuovo bel design, exhibition catalogue, Electa, Milan 1992.

Starck in Wien, exhibition catalogue, Die Kommode, Vienna 1992.

M.C. Tommasini and M. Pancera, *Il design italiano*, Mondadori, Milan 1992.

Var. Authors, *Carl Larsson*, Bokforlaget Bra Bocker, Göteborg 1992.

Var. Authors, *Objects and Images*, U.I.A.H., Helsinki 1992.

U. Brandes, *Richard Sapper* , Steidi, Göttingen 1993.

Brigitte Fitoussi, Objects Affectifs, Hazan, Paris 1993.

Cristina Morozzi, Massimo Morozzi, L'Archivolto, Milan 1993.

Design und Wohnen 2, exhibition catalogue, Helga Treft Verlag, Frankfurt 1993.

P. Dormer, *Design since 1945*, Thames and Hudson, London 1993.

H. Höger, *Ettore Sottsass Jun.*, Ernst Wasmuth, Berlin 1993.

Il design degli oggetti, exhibition catalogue, (Gallarate, Civica Galleria d'Arte Moderna), Gallarate 1993.

La fabbrica estetica, exhibition catalogue, ICE, Milan 1993.

Museum für Angewandte Kunst. Ein Wegweiser von A bis Z, Cologne 1993.

L. Polinoro, *Family Follows Fiction*, F.A.O., Crusinallo 1993.

S. Prinz, *Besteck des 20. Jahrhunderts*, Klinkhardt & Biermann, Munich 1993.

Sipek Borek, The International Design Yearbook , Rick Poynor, London 1993.

Var. Authors, *Modern Ad Art Museum*, Stern, Hamburg 1993.

Richard Sapper Design, exhibition catalogue, (Cologne, Museum für Angewandte Kunst), Cologne 1993.

M. Turinetto, *Dizionario del design*, Lupetti & C., Milan 1993.

Arts et formes ou 40 variations pour une histoire d'eau, exhibition catalogue (Pargi, Musée du Louvre), Paris 1994.

A. Buch and M. Vogt (edited by), *Janet Abrams, Laura Cerwinske, Michael Collins, Rainer Krause, Aldo Rossi, Michael Graves. Designer Monographs 3*, Vogt, Ernst & Son, Berlin 1994.

M. Byars, *The Design Encyclopedia*, Laurence King, London 1994.

F. Burkhardt, *Marco Zanuso*, Federico Motta, Milan 1994.

T. Heidert, M. Stegmann, and R. Zey, *Lexikon Intenationales Design*, Rowohlt, Hamburg 1994.

Le fabbriche del design italiano. Une dynastie d'objects Alessi, exhibition catalogue, Istituto Italiano Di Cultura, Paris 1994.

R. Poletti, *La cucina elettrica*, Electa-Alessi, Milan 1994.

Raymond Guidot, histoire du design 1940, Hazan, Paris 1994.

The International Design Yearbook 1994, Laurence King, London 1994.

Totocchio, exhibition catalogue, F&T Boo, Vicenza 1994.

O. Tusquets Blanca, *Mas que discutible*, Tusquets Editores, Barcelona 1994.

Var. Authors, *Alessi. The Design Factory*, Academy Group, London 1994.

Var. Authors, *Atelier Mendini. Una utopia visiva*, Fabbri, Milan 1994.

A La Castiglione, exhibition catalogue, Istituto Italiano di Cultura, Barcelona 1995.

Das International Design Jahrbuch 1994–1995, Bangert Verlag, Munich 1995.

XVII Premio Compasso d'oro, exhibition catalogue, Silvia Editrice, Milan 1995.

Oscar Tusquets Enric Miralles, exhibition catalogue, Tusquets Editores, Barcelona 1995.

A. Pansera, *Dizionario del design italiano*, Cantini, Milan 1995.

Pour un couteau. design et couverts 1970–1990, exhibition catalogue, Thiers 1995.

The Hannover Yearbook of Industrial Design, exhibition catalogue (Hannover, Industrial Forum Design), Hannover 1995.

The International Design Yearbook 1995, Laurence King Publishing, London 1995.

Thomas Haufe. Design, Dumont, Cologne 1995.

Torino design. Dall'automobile al cucchiaino, exhibition catalogue, Umberto Allemandi, Turin 1995.

Var. Authors, *Opere postume progettate in vita. Metallwerkstatt Bauhaus anni '20-anni '90*, Electa-Alessi, Milan 1995.

Alessandro Mendini 30 Colours, V+K Publishing, Bussum 1996.

Bella Forma, Landschaftverband Westfalen-Lippe, Hagen 1996.

A. Branzi, *Il design italiano 1964–1990*, exhibition catalogue, Electa, Milan 1996.

S. Casciani, *The Art Factory*, exhibition catalogue, Editrice Abitare Segesta, Milan 1996.

Fulvio Ferrari, Ettore Sottsass, tutta la ceramica, Umberto Allemandi, Turin 1996.

F. Haks, *Mendini*, Edizioni Archivolto, Milan 1996.

The International Design Yearbook 1996, Laurence King, London 1996.

M. Meneguzzo, *Philippe Starck distordre*, Electa-Alessi, Milan 1996.

M. Meuth and B. Neuner-Duttenhofer, *Piemont und Aostatal*, Droemer Knaur, Munich 1996.

A. Rossi, *Villa sul lago Maggiore*, Il Cardo, Venezia 1996.

P. Starck, *Vanity Case*, Taschen, Cologne 1996.

Var. Authors, *Design im Wandel*, Bangert Verlag, Bremen 1996.

Var. Authors, *Dictionnaire International des Arts Appliques et du Design*, Editions du Regard, Paris 1996.

Var. Authors, *L'oggetto dell'equilibrio*, Electa-Alessi, Milan 1996.

Werkzeuge. Design des Elementaren, Landesgalerie, Austria 1996.

G. Bertsch, *The Water Kettle by Michael Graves*, Verlag form, Frankfurt a.M. 1997.

F. Burkhardt and C. Morozzi, *Andrea Branzi*, Dis Voir, Paris 1997.

Gout Design, Musée de Louviers, Paris 1997.

S. Gronert, *The 9090 Cafetiere by Richard Sapper*, Verlag form, Frankfurt a.M. 1997.

A. Alessi, *La fabbrica dei sogni*, Electa, Milan 1998.

Industriedesign Igàr og Idag, Henie Onstad Kunstsenter, 1998.

C. Morozzi, *Oggetti risorti*, Costa&Nolan, Milan 1998.

The International Design Yearbook 1998, Laurence King Publishing, London 1998.

Alessi objects are in the collections of the following museums and public institutions

The Museum of Modern Art, New York; Louisiana Museum of Modern Art, Humlebaek; Museu de Arte, San Paolo; Die Neue Sammlung, Staatliches Museum für Angewandte Kunst, Munich; Kunstgewerbemuseum der Stadt Zürich, Zurich; Philadelphia Museum of Art, Philadelphia; Israel Museum, Jerusalem; The Metropolitan Museum of Art, New York; Museum Boymans-van-Beuningen, Rotterdam; Kunstgewerbemuseum SMPK, Berlin; Kunstmuseum, Düsseldorf; Minneapolis Institute of Art, Minneapolis; National Gallery of Victoria, Melbourne; Yale University Art Gallery, New Haven; National Museum of Modern Art, Kyoto; Bauhaus-Archiv Museum, Berlin; Bio Design Collection, Ljubljana; Kunstgewerbemuseum, Cologne; Ostfriesisches Tee-Museum, Norden; Victoria and Albert Museum, London; The Australian National Gallery, Canberra; Museum voor Sierkunst, Gand; Stedelijk Museum, Amsterdam; Groninger Museum, Groningen; Museum Folkwang, Essen; Museum für Angewandte Kunst, Cologne; Deutsches Klingenmuseum, Solingen; The Brooklyn Museum, New York; Les Musées des Arts Décoratifs, Paris; Museum of Applied Arts, Helsinki; The Denver Art Museum, Denver; Museo de Artes Decorativas, Barcelona; Henie Instad Art Center Kunstsenterhovikodden, Norway.

Photograph Credits

Alessi Archives, Arici and Bernardi, Atelier Mendini
Archives, Aldo and Marirosa Ballo, Maria Vittoria Backaus,
Bauhaus Archiv, Raffaello Benedetti Bra, Giovanni Berengo
Gardin, Bergamo and Basso, Riccardo Bianchi, Andrea
Branzi Archives, Luigi Brenna, Santi Caleca, Franco Capra,
Riccardo Dalisi Archives, Attilio Del Comune, Eurostand
Archives, Florence Gift Mart Archives, Fotorama, Enzo
Franza, Giacomo Giannini, Stefano Giovannoni Archives,
Michael Graves Archives, Pino Guidolotti, J. King, Stefan
Kirchner, Mattew Klein, Carlo Lavatori, Lucio Lazzara,
Salvatore Licitra, Mauro Masera, Jean Baptiste Mondino,
Occhiomagico, Carlo Paggiarino, Sergio Pancaldi, Giuseppe
Pino, Franco Sargiani, Renato Sartori, Oliver Schuh and
Barbara Burg, Luciano Soave, Sottsass Associati Archives,
Studio Azzurro, Top Studio di Zappalà, Leo Torri, Oliviero
Toscani, Emilio Tremolada, Franco Uberti, Tom Vack,
Guido Venturini Archives, Walter Zerla. Illustrations
by Libero Gozzini and Wilma Incerti, Studio Softroom,
Suresh Sethi, Tiger Tateishi.

Holders of rights to any unidentified photographic material
are invited to bring the matter to the attention
of the originating publishers.

This volume was printed
by Arnoldo Mondadori Editore S.p.A., Verona,
on behalf of Elemond S.p.A. in 1999